Disclaimer

The information contained in this book is for educational and informational purposes only and is not intended as medical, psychological, or professional advice. The content is not a substitute for professional medical advice, diagnosis, or treatment from a qualified healthcare provider or mental health professional.

Dr. Vivian Tantoh Mondo is a licensed psychiatric nurse practitioner, but the relationship between the author and readers of this book does not constitute a doctor-patient relationship. The strategies, suggestions, and techniques discussed in this book are offered as general information and should not be treated as personalized medical or psychological advice.

Always seek the advice of your physician, psychiatrist, psychologist, or other qualified healthcare provider with any questions you may have regarding a medical condition, mental health concern, or treatment options. Never disregard professional medical advice or delay seeking treatment because of something you have read in this book.

The author and publisher make no representations or warranties with respect to the accuracy, applicability, fitness, or completeness of the contents of this book. They disclaim any warranties (express or implied), merchantability, or fitness for any particular purpose. The author and publisher shall in no event be held liable for any loss or other damages, including but not limited to special, incidental, consequential, or other damages.

Individual results may vary. The testimonials and examples used throughout this book are not intended to represent or guarantee that anyone will achieve the same or similar results.

The use of this book implies your acceptance of this disclaimer.

Dr. Vivian Tantoh Mondo, DNP

Embracing Your Authentic Self

The Journey to True Freedom—
Silence Your Inner Critic,
Love Your Flaws, Live Boldly

ISBN Electronic: # 979-8-9993698-1-9
ISBN Paperback: # 979-8-9993698-0-2
ISBN Hardcover: # 979-8-9993698-2-6
Library of Congress Control Number: # 2025915663

Publishing Consultant: PRESStinely, PRESStinely.com

Portions of this book are works of nonfiction. Certain names and identifying characteristics have been changed.

Printed in the United States of America.

Dr. Vivian Tantoh Mondo, DNP
DrVivianMondo.com

This book is dedicated to the greatest Physician I know - Jesus Christ.

*Through His faithfulness, I am able to fulfill this assignment,
and for that, I am eternally grateful.*

*Every insight and piece of wisdom shared within these pages was
divinely inspired. The Holy Spirit was my guide, teacher, and source -
faithfully leading me through every word and chapter.*

To Him be all the glory.

~

*To my late parents, **Tantoh John and Tantoh Scholastica**,*

and my late maternal grandmother,
Mama Veronica Sangbong Ayah—

*your love, wisdom, and resilience have shaped my journey in
countless ways.*

*When all hope is lost, I pull from your stories and find the faith to
take another step.*

Your sacrifices, guidance, and unwavering spirit continue to inspire me.

This book is a tribute to your enduring legacy.

Table of Contents

Acknowledgments

*F*irst and foremost, I want to express my heartfelt gratitude to
You, the reader, for choosing to walk this journey to freedom
with me. I would not write this book if not for you.

Writing *Embracing Your Authentic Self: A Journey to True Freedom*
has been a profoundly transformative experience. This book
represents more than my journey; it is a culmination of countless
moments, insights, and the unwavering support of those who have
walked this path with me. My heart overflows with gratitude to all
who have been part of this journey.

My deepest gratitude goes to my family. To my amazing husband,
Pastor Mondo—your steadfast faith and unwavering encouragement
have been my anchor, grounding me through every step of this
journey. Your love and partnership have been instrumental in
bringing this vision to life.

To my three beautiful children, **Isaiah, Lizzy, and Baby Miracle
Light**—your curiosity, resilience, and boundless love remind me
daily of life's most precious gifts. You are the light illuminating my
path, inspiring me to keep going.

I owe immense gratitude to my parents, whose lives were
testaments to perseverance, integrity, and selflessness. My late
mother, whose memory is a constant source of strength and
inspiration, continues to drive me forward. Your unwavering belief
in my potential continues to inspire me. Every page of this book
carries a piece of your legacy. To my siblings and extended family,

thank you for believing in me and cheering me on every step of the way.

To my professional colleagues, Dr. Abraham Ayodele, MD, thank you for the foreword, and to my mentor, NP Charles Edner, in psychiatric nursing, I am forever grateful for your wisdom, encouragement, and shared dedication to this transformative work. Your insights have enriched this book and shaped my understanding in ways I could not have achieved alone.

To my dear friends, especially Ms. Andrea Macoy and the members of our faith community, your prayers, kind words, and unwavering belief in this project have strengthened me during moments of doubt. Your support demonstrates the power of connection and shared faith.

I want to extend a heartfelt thank you to my dear friend and big sister, Dr. Nicoline Ambe, for your unwavering support and constant encouragement through the years. Your gentle reminders and belief in me helped turn this dream into a reality.

To my editorial team, Sherry L. Granader and Emmanuel, thank you for your diligence, expertise, and dedication to excellence. Your attention to detail, from editing and formatting to re-editing, and your ability to enhance my vision have been invaluable in making sure this book resonates with readers on every level. Your patience and steadfast commitment did not go unnoticed.

To my wonderful publishers, Kristen Kasza-Wise and Maira Pedierra of PRESStinely - thank you for working tirelessly behind the scenes. Despite my many mind shifts and constant changes, you never grew tired or annoyed. Your dedication, grace, and professionalism are truly a gift.

To everyone who has played a part in this journey, whether through moments of encouragement, shared laughter, or quiet reflection, you have been a beacon of light guiding me toward the realization of this journey.

Thank you for believing in the power of authenticity and for walking alongside me on this journey to freedom. Together, we continue to create a world where living authentically is celebrated and everyone feels empowered to embrace their truest self.

Foreword

By Dr. Abraham Ayodele, MD
Board-Certified Psychiatrist | Mentor | Former Colleague at Dallas Behavioral Hospital

W hen Dr. Vivian Tantoh Mondo asked me to write the foreword for her upcoming book, *Embracing Your Authentic Self: A Journey to True Freedom*, I felt both honored and deeply moved. As a psychiatrist with decades of clinical experience, I've worked with many exceptional professionals, but very few leave the kind of lasting impact that Vivian has made on me and on countless others.

Our paths crossed while working together at Dallas Behavioral Hospital. From our very first encounter, I recognized her rare blend of clinical skill, emotional intelligence, and spiritual insight. She was not only a gifted psychiatric nurse but a compassionate leader with a calming presence and a deep commitment to holistic healing. It's no surprise that she's now taken her message beyond the hospital walls into the hearts and homes of readers everywhere.

Embracing Your Authentic Self is much more than a self-help book. It is a deeply personal, spiritually grounded, and psychologically rich guide for anyone who longs to break free from fear, shame, and the expectations of others. Dr. Mondo leads the reader gently—but boldly—into a journey of returning to one's God-given identity.

With the voice of a clinician, the heart of a pastor's wife, and the honesty of someone who has walked this path herself, she uncovers what so many silently battle: perfectionism, people-pleasing, insecurity, and inner criticism. Yet, instead of just naming these struggles, she helps readers overcome them—layer by layer—with grace, wisdom, and practical tools.

What sets this book apart is its unique integration of therapeutic insight and spiritual truth. Vivian draws from her own lived experiences, her clinical background, and her strong faith to offer readers more than information—she offers transformation. Through engaging stories, reflection questions, and scriptural truth, she equips her readers to do the sacred work of healing from the inside out.

One of the core messages of the book is that freedom doesn't come from striving to become someone you're not—but from returning to who you were created to be. That message is both liberating and deeply needed in our world today.

For mental health professionals, this book will serve as a refreshing reminder of why we do what we do. For spiritual seekers, it is an invitation to anchor your healing in divine truth. For anyone wrestling with identity, shame, or burnout, this book is a lifeline.

Reading *Embracing Your Authentic Self* reminded me that healing is not just about managing symptoms—it's about reclaiming wholeness. Vivian's words carry both strength and gentleness, conviction and compassion. Her message challenged me to reflect more deeply on the masks we all wear and the freedom that awaits when we finally let them go.

Anyone who is looking to overcome self-doubt, heal emotional wounds, or simply live more authentically will find rich wisdom and practical guidance in this book. Dr. Mondo does not just teach authenticity—she embodies it.

I am incredibly proud of the work Vivian has done in these pages. As her former colleague and mentor, I have seen firsthand the power of her voice, her story, and her unwavering commitment to helping others live in truth. This book is the natural extension of the life she lives—and it is a gift to every person who picks it up.

So, take a deep breath. Open your heart. And prepare to be challenged, empowered, and set free.

Dr. Abraham Ayodele, MD
Dallas, Texas

Preface

There comes a moment in every life when the masks we've worn begin to feel too heavy. When the noise of expectation, trauma, culture, and comparison drowns out the gentle whisper of who we truly are. I wrote this book for that moment.

Embracing Your Authentic Self: The Power to True Freedom is more than a title, it's a personal revolution. It is born from my own journey as a woman, a mother, a psychiatric nurse practitioner, a pastor's wife, and a servant leader to both my local community and the nations. I've sat with broken hearts and resilient spirits. I've walked the roads of healing and seen what it takes to step out of survival and into significance.

Through my practice at Arise and Shine Health Center, my work with Light of the World Ministry Network alongside my husband, and our outreach efforts to hospitals, prisons, and orphanages across Africa and the Caribbean, I have learned one universal truth: You can't truly serve or soar while hiding behind someone else's version of you.

This book is a call to freedom. Not just emotional or spiritual freedom, but the liberating power of truth, identity, and alignment. It's about removing the layers, healing the wounds, and learning to show up boldly in the world as the woman or man God intended you to be.

As you turn these pages, you will be invited to confront lies, break cycles, and reclaim your voice. You'll explore practical tools, soul-nourishing truths, and real-life stories meant to ignite the light within you.

I dedicate this work to every person who has ever felt unseen, unheard, or unworthy. You are not alone and you are not forgotten.

To my homeland, Cameroon, where our school project is rising from the soil, and to every young girl and boy watching with hope in their eyes—may this book remind you: your true power lies in your authentic self.

Let's walk this journey together. Because freedom is not found in perfection. It's found in truth.

With all my heart,
Dr. Vivian Tantoh Mondo

Introduction

Imagine waking up each day with a deep, unshakeable peace, knowing that every choice you make and every word you speak flows from your innermost truth. Picture living a life not dictated by the expectations of others but guided by the unique light within you. This is the power of authenticity—a life in harmony with your inner self, where your actions reflect your deepest values. It is a life of freedom, fulfilment, and profound connection.

For many, this may seem like a distant dream. We often wear masks to blend in, striving to meet society's standards and pursuing ideals that leave us feeling hollow. We suppress our true selves out of fear—fear of rejection, failure, and inadequacy. Over time, these fears create barriers, preventing us from living the lives we were truly meant to lead.

What if you could break through those barriers? What if you could rediscover the person you've always been, free from the limitations of fear and doubt? Imagine standing in the world not as a fragmented version of yourself but as a vibrant, whole individual—unapologetically you. This is the journey we are about to embark on together.

Why Authenticity Matters

Living authentically is more than just a path to personal happiness; it's the gateway to a life of true meaning. When we embrace who we truly are, we unlock the power to:

- Cultivate more profound, more meaningful relationships.

- Overcome the fears and doubts that hold us back.
- Make decisions that align with our deepest values and passions.
- Find lasting peace and purpose, even in a chaotic world.

Authenticity is a gift—not only to yourself but also to those around you. As you embrace your authentic self, you inspire others to do the same. You become a beacon of courage, demonstrating that it's okay to live fully as they are, imperfections and all. When we contemplate authenticity as a gift, we can grasp it on multiple levels that interweave both personal growth and social awareness connection.

At its core, authenticity means allowing our true selves to be visible to the world - our genuine thoughts, feelings, and experiences without artificial filters or personas. This requires tremendous courage because it involves being vulnerable and accepting that not everyone will appreciate or understand our authentic selves.

However, why is this a gift? First, consider how it benefits us: When we live authentically, we free up the mental and emotional energy that would otherwise be spent maintaining facades. This creates space for genuine growth, creativity, and deeper self-understanding. We can direct our focus toward meaningful pursuits rather than on impression management.

Giving to others is equally powerful but operates through different mechanisms. When we are authentic, we grant others implicit permission to do the same. Consider it a safe harbor by demonstrating that we accept and express our truth; we signal to others that they can trust us with theirs. This catalyzes deeper, more meaningful relationships based on mutual understanding rather than superficial connections and interactions.

We can also consider authenticity as a gift through the lens of social learning. When we observe others navigating life authentically - including their struggles, uncertainties, and triumphs -

we learn from their genuine experiences rather than their curated presentations. This is especially powerful because authentic behavior often uncovers the messy yet important process of growth, not just the polished outcomes.

The metaphor of authenticity as a gift also hints at something significant about its nature: like any true gift, authentic behavior is not transactional. We don't act authentically to receive something in return. The benefits to us and others arise organically from the practice itself.

Reflection Questions:

- *What aspects of authenticity as a gift resonate most with your experience?*
- *Have you observed specific ways that authentic behavior creates positive ripple effects in your relationships or community?*
- *What do you like about your authentic self?*

The Journey Ahead

This book serves as both a guide and a companion on your journey to embracing your authentic self. Divided into four parts, it presents practical tools, profound insights, and personal stories to support your exploration growth:

- **Understanding Your Authentic Self:** Explore the foundation of who you are, shedding layers of societal conditioning to reveal the values that define your core.
- **Overcoming Barriers to Authenticity:** Confront the fears and self-doubt that have held you back, replacing them with courage, confidence, and self-compassion.
- **Cultivating Self-Awareness and Embracing Vulnerability:** Learn to listen to your inner voice, embrace your imperfections, and express your true self in ways that foster deeper connections with others.

- **Living Authentically in the World:** Discover how to navigate challenges and setbacks while staying true to yourself, creating a life of purpose and fulfilment.

A Personal Invitation

As I write these words, I reflect on my journey toward authenticity. I've faced doubts about whether my voice mattered, wondering if I could truly be myself without fear of rejection. I have walked through loss, self-doubt, and perfectionism—and emerged with a deeper understanding of what it means to live authentically. This book reflects what I've learned and shared in the hope that it will light your way as you walk your path.

You are not alone on this journey. Every story, every exercise, and every insight in these pages is designed to empower you to embrace your authentic self with courage and compassion. The road to authenticity is not always easy but profoundly rewarding. With each step, you'll uncover the freedom, joy, and peace from aligning your life with who you truly are.

Are You Ready?

The journey to authenticity begins with a simple yet powerful choice: to say "yes" to yourself, your dreams, your values, and your unique voice. Embrace the freedom of living a life that is true to your essence.

Take a deep breath, open your heart, and step into this transformative journey. Together, we will peel back the layers, break through the barriers, and embrace the beauty of your authentic self.

This is your story. Your journey. Your freedom.

Let's begin.

Part 1:
Understanding Your Authentic Self

Chapter 1

Unveiling the Illusion of Perfection

We've all been there. That constant, nagging pressure to be perfect. The world tells us that to be loved and worthy, we must look a certain way, act a certain way, and live a certain way. The carefully curated lives on social media, the flawless appearances we see in the workplace, and even the expectations of the people closest to us—everything seems to scream that perfection is the goal.

However, what if I told you that this relentless chase for perfection isn't only impossible; it's also holding you back from embracing the real, authentic version of yourself? You see, perfection is a lie. It's a mirage, always just out of reach, teasing you with the idea that if you could just do one more thing—look a little better, work a little harder, be a little smarter—then you'd finally feel like you're enough. But the truth is, it never works that way. You're constantly chasing something that doesn't exist, and along the way, you lose sight of who you truly are.

The truth is that God, in His infinite wisdom, didn't create us to be perfect. Psalm 139:14 states, *"I praise you because I am fearfully and wonderfully made; your works are wonderful, I know that full well."* You are already wonderfully made, just as you are, with all your quirks and imperfections. It's the pressure to be something you're not that clouds your vision and keeps you stuck.

The Perfection Trap

I know this struggle all too well. For years, I let perfectionism rule my life. Every decision and every action was fuelled by the belief that I had to meet some invisible standard of perfection. If I didn't, I would face rejection. I would be a failure. It didn't matter how much I accomplished; the satisfaction was always short-lived because I wasn't measuring up to that ever-moving target. I felt like I was running on a treadmill, constantly moving but getting nowhere. And the more I tried, the more exhausted I became unfulfilled.

But one day, it hit me like a ton of bricks—what if perfection was the problem? What if my constant striving was the very thing that kept me from living authentically? The scripture from Philippians 1:6 reminds us, *"Being confident of this, that he who began a good work in you will carry it on to completion until the day of Christ Jesus."* You don't have to be perfect now because God is working in you. The work He started in you is ongoing, and there's no rush to figure it all out today.

Breaking Free from the Illusion

Letting go of perfection doesn't happen overnight, but it is achievable. The first step is recognizing that perfection doesn't exist. Once you let go of that belief, you'll be able to accept yourself—flaws, mistakes, and all. The journey to authenticity begins with self-acceptance. Progress is a better indicator than perfection. It shows that we are learning, growing, and working to become better versions of ourselves. Aim for excellence, not for an impossible ideal.

The Science Behind Perfectionism and Mental Well-being

Psychological research supports the idea that perfectionism is not only an illusion but also a significant barrier to mental health. Studies have shown that individuals with high levels of perfectionism are more prone to anxiety, depression, and burnout. According to a study published in *Psychological Bulletin*, perfectionism has been linked to increased levels of psychological distress, with socially prescribed perfectionism—when people feel external pressure to be perfect—is the most damaging.

Dr. Brené Brown, a researcher known for her work on vulnerability and self-worth, explains that perfectionism is a defense mechanism, an attempt to avoid shame and judgment. However, rather than protecting us, it isolates us. When we fear making mistakes, we hesitate to take risks, form meaningful connections, and fully experience life.

Moreover, neuroscience suggests that the constant stress caused by perfectionism activates the body's fight-or-flight response, leading to higher cortisol levels (the stress hormone). Over time, this can negatively impact both physical and mental health, contributing to exhaustion, chronic fatigue, and even cardiovascular issues.

However, there is hope. Studies on self-compassion, led by psychologist Dr. Kristin Neff, indicate that those who practice self-kindness rather than harsh self-criticism experience lower levels of stress and higher levels of resilience. Instead of striving for an unattainable ideal, embracing our imperfections allows us to grow in a healthier, more fulfilling way.

So, as you begin your journey toward authenticity, remember: Perfection is not the goal—growth is. Science and faith alike remind us that true peace comes not from flawless performance but from embracing who we are, just as we are. And that is more than enough.

I'm not saying it's easy. It takes practice, patience, and a shift in how you see yourself. But trust me, it's worth it. You'll start to experience freedom—the freedom to fail, to grow, to learn, and to be unapologetically YOU.

Here's how you can start breaking free:

1. **Reframe Your Inner Dialogue:** Pay attention to how you speak to yourself. When that harsh inner critic starts whispering that you are not enough, ask yourself, "Would I say this to a friend?" Replace negative self-talk with compassion. For example, instead of thinking, *"I'm such a failure for making that mistake,"* try telling yourself, *"Everyone makes mistakes. This is an opportunity to learn and grow."*

2. **Set Realistic Expectations:** Perfection doesn't mean doing everything flawlessly; it means doing the best you can with what you have. Set realistic goals that encourage progress, not unattainable perfection.

3. **Learn From Mistakes:** Mistakes are not a sign of failure. They are part of the learning process. When something doesn't go as planned, ask yourself, *"What can I learn from this?"*

4. **Celebrate Your Uniqueness:** Instead of trying to fit into someone else's mold, celebrate the qualities that make you uniquely you. Your quirks, your struggles, your journey—all of it makes you who you are.

5. **Limit Comparisons:** Social media has a way of showing only the best parts of people's lives. Remind yourself that there's more to the story than what's posted online. Take a break from scrolling and permit yourself to live in your own reality.

6. **Practice Gratitude:** When you focus on what you're thankful for, it shifts your perspective. Gratitude allows you to see the beauty in the present moment, not just in some far-off future where everything is "perfect."

The Beauty of Imperfection

Once you begin to let go of the lie of perfection, something magical happens. You find peace in your imperfections. You stop trying to be someone you're not and start fully embracing who you are. The more you accept yourself, the more you unlock the ability to connect deeply with others.

Remember, living authentically doesn't mean being flawless; it means being real. When you are real, you also create space for others to be real. And that's where the magic happens. Just as it's written in Philippians 1:6, *"Being confident of this, that he who began a good work in you will carry it on to completion..."* Your journey is unfolding step by step, and each step is a step toward a more authentic version of yourself.

Reflection Question:

What aspects of finding peace with imperfections would you like to explore more deeply?

To cultivate a more authentic self, regularly ask yourself questions that explore your values, desires, fears, and the gap between your actions and your true self. Examples include: "What are my core values?", "What brings me genuine joy?", "What am I most afraid of?", and "What would I do if I weren't afraid?"

Reflecting on these questions can help you identify and address discrepancies between your perceived self and your authentic self, ultimately leading to more genuine and fulfilling living.

Chapter 2

Deconstructing Conditioning

From the moment we take our first breath, we begin absorbing messages about who we should be and how we should live. These messages come from everywhere: our families, the surrounding culture, society, and even religion. They function like invisible scripts, shaping our thoughts, behaviors, and sense of self, often without us even realizing it. Some of these influences are helpful, guiding us toward positive growth, while others can feel like heavy chains, confining us to an identity that doesn't truly fit.

I know because I've been there. I've spent a large part of my life trying to fit into molds that were never mine, and it wasn't until I started peeling back the layers of conditioning that I realized how much of my identity had been shaped by external forces. I grew up hearing messages about who I was supposed to be, what success looked like, and how to behave to be accepted. But over time, I began to wonder: Is this really me, or is this just a role I've been playing for someone else script?

In this chapter, we will examine the layers of conditioning in more detail. We will explore their origins, how they have influenced our lives, and how we can begin to question and release them. This isn't about rejecting everything we have learned; it is about discerning what aligns with our true selves and what no longer serves us.

The Weight of Conditioning

Let me take you back to my childhood. Growing up in a family that valued hard work and achievement, I was consistently praised for being the "responsible one," the one who followed the rules and did everything right. My parents, with the best of intentions, encouraged me to excel in all my endeavors—be it school, sports, or even friendships. They meant well, but their expectations of perfection influenced how I viewed myself. If I didn't succeed, I felt as though I was letting everyone down.

Now, imagine attempting to bear all that weight day after day, convinced that your worth was linked to your accomplishments. That was me for years—trapped in a cycle of evaluating myself by external standards. At the time, it felt as though I was walking a tightrope, perpetually fearful that one wrong move would make me fall.

But then, something shifted. I began to feel the weight of those expectations pressing down on me, and I started asking myself, *"Is this really who I am?"*

The turning point came when I faced a major decision in my life. I had a job offer on the table that promised security and success in the eyes of others, but deep down, I knew it wasn't the right path for me. I thought about how my parents would react and how society would view me if I chose a different route. That's when I realized—the weight of other people's expectations was holding me back from embracing the person I was meant to be.

It felt as if the words from Romans 12:2 suddenly made sense to me: "Do not conform to the pattern of this world but be transformed by the renewing of your mind." I had been conforming to a world that wasn't mine, and it was time to renew my mind and embrace a life that felt true to who I was.

Understanding Your Conditioning

The first step in breaking free from conditioning is awareness. Often, we don't even realize that we've adopted beliefs and behaviors that aren't truly ours. We've been operating on autopilot, following the script we were given. But here's the good news—once you become aware of these influences, you can start choosing what remains and what can be let go.

Step 1: Identify the Sources

Consider the significant influences in your life. Where did you receive the messages that shaped your sense of self? Was it from your family, your culture, or society? For me, growing up, I internalized messages like, "You must achieve to be worthy," and "Don't rock the boat—always make everyone happy." These beliefs were handed down from my parents, reinforced by the culture I lived in, and further emphasized by society's constant messages about success and image. Looking back, I recognize how much these beliefs limited me. They compelled me to strive for perfection and avoid conflict, even when it meant disregarding my feelings and needs.

Action Step: Write down the key sources of influence in your life and the messages you absorbed. Ask yourself:

- What did I learn from my family?
- How did my cultural background shape who I became?
- What societal pressures influenced my decisions and self-image?

Step 2: Examine Your Beliefs

Once you've identified those sources, begin examining the beliefs that originated from them. Are they still true for you? Do they support your growth, or are they holding you back?

I held the belief that I needed to be constantly agreeable to avoid disappointing others. For a long time, I thought it was just part of who I was until I realized it stemmed from childhood. When I was praised for being "good" and not causing disruptions, I adopted the belief that I had to always say "yes" to maintain the peace. However, as I grew older, I started to see how this belief forced me to suppress my own voice and needs.

Action Step: Reflect on the beliefs you've picked up along the way. Are they really yours? Do they serve you, or are they holding you back?

Step 3: Notice Patterns

Conditioning often shows up in recurring patterns. Reflect on your habits and automatic responses. Do you avoid conflict because you were always taught to keep the peace? Do you over-apologize, even when you're not in the wrong?

Example: I noticed that I'd avoid speaking up in meetings or sharing my true opinion because I was taught that disagreement meant disrespect. It took time, but eventually, I learned that my voice mattered—whether it fit the mold of "polite" or "agreeable."

Step 4: Challenge Limiting Beliefs

Once you've identified the beliefs that no longer serve you, it's time to challenge them. Ask yourself: What evidence supports this belief? What might occur if I let it go? For example, I used to believe that I needed to achieve perfection to be loved. However, as I examined my life, I realized that I was already loved for who I was—flaws and all.

Action Step: Choose a limiting belief and reframe it. If you've always believed you must be perfect to be worthy of love, try replacing it with: *"I am worthy of love just as I am, imperfections included."*

Step 5: Experiment with New Behaviors

Start small. Practice saying "no" when you've always said "yes" to please others. Notice how it feels when you honor your own needs. This isn't about being selfish—it's about being authentic.

Example: The next time someone asks you for something, pause and consider, "Do I really want to do this?" Practice saying "no" when it doesn't align with your values, and observe how your sense of self becomes stronger.

Peeling Back the Layers

Deconstructing conditioning isn't about throwing everything away. It's about peeling back the layers of expectations and discovering what is truly yours. It takes time and patience, but with each layer you shed, you uncover more of who you are meant to be.

Remember, you've always had everything you need inside of you. The journey is about rediscovering that truth. That is what I will help you do as your coach.

The Role of Mindfulness in Releasing Conditioning

Mindfulness practices, including meditation and self-reflection, have been shown to enhance self-awareness and diminish the influence of conditioned responses. When individuals engage in mindfulness, they learn to observe their thoughts and emotions without immediate reaction, creating space between stimulus and response. This allows for more intentional decision-making instead of automatic adherence to conditioned behaviors.

Mindfulness meditation leads to structural changes in the brain, particularly in the prefrontal cortex (associated with decision-making) and the amygdala (linked to fear and emotional processing).

These changes empower individuals to break free from conditioned fear responses and develop greater autonomy over their thoughts and actions.

Rewriting the Narrative

Our personal narrative shapes our identity. In other words, we can rewrite our life story to align with our true values. When we view our conditioned beliefs as distinct entities rather than a permanent part of our identity, we can dismantle limiting beliefs.

Psychological research suggests that personal narratives shape identity (McAdams, 1993). When individuals deconstruct conditioning, they essentially rewrite their life stories to reflect their true values. Narrative therapy, a therapeutic approach developed by Michael White and David Epston (1990), helps individuals separate themselves from societal and familial scripts, empowering them to craft self-authored narratives.

A key technique in narrative therapy is *externalization*, where individuals learn to see conditioned beliefs as separate entities rather than integral parts of their identity. This shift fosters the ability to question and dismantle limiting beliefs while reinforcing self-defined values.

Empowerment Through Awareness and Action

Scientific evidence supports the idea that deconstructing conditioning is both possible and transformative. Through neuroplasticity, CBT, mindfulness, and narrative therapy, individuals can break free from inherited limitations and develop a more authentic, self-directed existence. The process requires consistent effort, but research confirms that identity is not fixed—it evolves as we actively engage in self-reflection, critical thinking, and intentional behavioral change.

By integrating these evidence-based strategies, individuals can step into a life that is truly their own, grounded in authenticity rather than external expectations.

Exercise: Timeline of Influences

Create a timeline of your life. For each significant event, reflect on the messages you received about how you "should" be. How do these messages influence your behavior today?

Example: Starting school.
Message: "Good kids follow the rules."
Impact: I struggle to take risks or challenge authority, even when it's necessary.

Mindfulness Integration

Whenever a limiting belief arises, take a moment to pause and breathe:

- Close your eyes.
- Take three deep breaths, focusing on the sensation of air entering and leaving your body.
- Acknowledge the belief without judgment: "I see you, but you no longer control me."
- Return to the present moment, knowing that you are in control of your own story.

Key Takeaway

Recognizing and deconstructing conditioning allows you to reclaim your true, authentic self. By questioning old beliefs and behaviors, you can create space for growth, freedom, and alignment with who you truly are, no longer living according to someone else's script.

Hopefully, you now have a clearer picture of your most authentic self and are feeling excited to step into this version of you! I acknowledge that this process isn't always easy, so I encourage you to reflect on what's currently holding you back from embracing this badass version of yourself. This should give you an idea of small changes you can start making to break down these barriers.

Chapter 3

Discovering Your Core Values

As you stand at the crossroads of life, imagine an inner voice whispering: *"The path you choose reflects the treasure within your heart."* This treasure is not material wealth or worldly acclaim—it is the essence of your being, the profound principles illuminating your way forward. These principles are your core values and hold the key to a life of clarity, joy, and profound fulfilment.

Your core values are like seeds planted in the fertile soil of your subconscious mind. When nurtured, they grow into a flourishing life of purpose and harmony. However, if ignored, they lie dormant, leaving you adrift and disconnected from your true self. To live authentically, you must uncover these values, for they reveal the desires of your heart and the divine direction of your life.

The Power of Core Values

Every choice you make is like a magnet drawing experiences into your life. When your choices align with your core values, you feel a sense of peace, knowing that you are moving in harmony with the infinite intelligence within. When misaligned, however, life may feel turbulent, as though you are swimming against the current of your inner truth. Your core values act as a compass, guiding you back to the center of your being, where clarity and wisdom reside.

How do you discover these guiding principles? The answer lies in the power of reflection, an inner journey that taps into the subconscious mind, the great storehouse of divine wisdom.

Unveiling Your Core Values

The process of uncovering your core values is a sacred act of self-discovery. Through quiet reflection, you awaken to the desires planted by divine inspiration within your heart.

Begin with these steps:

1. **Recall Moments of Joy and Fulfillment**
   Reflect on experiences that filled you with a sense of aliveness and joy. These moments reveal the values that were being honored. When you feel a deep sense of satisfaction, it is a sign that you are in tune with your divine blueprint.

2. **Notice Feelings of Resistance**
   Recall times when life felt stagnant or dissatisfying. These moments are not failures but signals, alerting you to areas where your values were suppressed or ignored. Such awareness is a gift, for it guides you back to alignment.

3. **Admire the Qualities You Honor in Others**
   The attributes you admire in others are reflections of the values that reside within you. As you recognize these qualities, affirm their presence in your own life, and see how they shape your destiny.

Integrating Your Values into Daily Life

Once you have identified your core values, the next step is to infuse them into your everyday choices. Aligning with your values means aligning with the divine energy flowing through you, bringing about a life of purpose and peace.

- **Decision-Making with Purpose**
  When faced with choices, ask yourself: *"Does this align with the treasure within my heart?"* Let your values illuminate your path, ensuring each step resonates with your higher self.

- **Setting Intentions with Clarity**
  Every goal you set becomes a channel through which your values are expressed. If growth is a core value, commit to learning something new daily. If compassion is your guiding principle, seek ways to uplift and serve those around you.

- **Building Boundaries with Confidence**
  Honor your values by setting boundaries that protect them. If balance is essential, safeguard your time and energy from unnecessary distractions. In doing so, you affirm your worth and align your life with divine order.

Practical Exercises for Alignment

Here is a simple yet powerful exercise to deepen your connection to your core values:

1. Sit in a quiet place and close your eyes. Take a few deep breaths, allowing your mind to relax.
2. Visualize a moment in your life when you felt truly alive and at peace. Allow this memory to unfold in your mind and notice the feelings it brings.
3. Ask yourself: *"What value was I honoring in that moment?"* Trust the answer that arises, for it is a whisper from your subconscious mind.
4. Repeat this process daily, affirming the values you uncover and integrating them into your life with intention.

The Truth Within

The world does not impose your core values—they are gifts from within, treasures that reflect the divine spark in you. When you honor them, you align with the infinite intelligence of your subconscious mind, drawing harmony and abundance into your life.

Let these truths guide you: as you embrace your heart's desires, you are living authentically and fulfilling the divine plan inscribed upon your soul. Trust in this inner guidance and observe how the world transforms to reflect the light of your deepest values. Listening to your inner guidance creates a life that resonates with your heart and soul.

Every step you take feels more intentional and meaningful because it's guided by who you are at your core, rather than by what others expect. This alignment with your inner self allows you to experience life more fully, handle challenges with resilience, and find joy in unexpected places. You're no longer living by someone else's script; you're tuning into your own rhythm, one that reflects the real you.

Dare to trust your heart and live in alignment with your truest self. Embrace the magic that resides in the unknown and allow yourself to be guided by your inner wisdom. By following your heart, you not only transform your own life—you also inspire others to live fully and authentically, creating a world where we can all shine in our unique ways.

Part 2

Overcoming Barriers to Authenticity

Chapter 4

Confronting Fear and Self-Doubt

Fear and self-doubt are like shadows on the path to authenticity, often appearing when you're about to enter a new realm of possibility. Yet, though unsettling, these feelings can become powerful tools for growth when approached with the right mindset. As you walk this journey, remember that fear and self-doubt are not enemies but signals—a reminder that you are stepping into uncharted territory.

The Nature of Fear and Self-Doubt

Fear and self-doubt arise from layers of past experiences, societal pressures, and internal beliefs. These layers can weigh on your spirit, whispering that you're incapable, unworthy, or insufficient. However, beneath these whispers lies a profound truth: these feelings only hold power when you grant them that authority.

Consider moments when fear held you back or when self-doubt silenced your voice. Each of those moments was an invitation to turn inward, reflect, and recalibrate. Please recognize that these emotions do not define you; they merely indicate areas where your inner potential is ready to emerge.

Transforming Negative Self-Talk

Negative self-talk is one of the most pervasive barriers to authenticity. It may sound like:

- "I'm not skilled enough."
- "What if I fail and everyone sees?"
- "I'm worthless."

Each time you entertain such thoughts; you reinforce a false narrative. Instead, challenge these internal voices by asking:

- Is this thought based on truth or fear?
- What would I say to a dear friend in this situation?
- What evidence exists that contradicts this belief?

Replace the narrative with affirming truths about yourself. For example:

Negative Thought: "I'll fail if I try something new."
Reframe: "Every new step brings lessons that prepare me for success."

Building Self-Confidence Step by Step

Self-confidence isn't granted to a select few; it's cultivated through consistent action. Like planting seeds, you nurture them with daily effort, trust, and patience.

1. **Set Small, Achievable Goals**
   Break larger tasks into manageable steps. Each completed step builds momentum and reinforces your belief in yourself.

   Example: If public speaking scares you, start by sharing your ideas in a small group before addressing a larger audience.

2. **Celebrate Progress**
   Every small victory deserves acknowledgment. Celebrate not just the outcome but also the courage it took to try.

Example: Completing a project, even with imperfections, is a step closer to mastery.

3. **Prioritize Self-Care**
   Your mind and body are interconnected. Nurturing your well-being reinforces your inner strength and resilience.

   Example: Practice mindfulness, exercise regularly, and rest when needed.

Courageously Stepping Toward Authenticity

Authenticity means acting in alignment with your true self, even when facing fear. This courage is cultivated gradually as you push beyond your comfort zone. The good news is that discovering the autonomy of courage is liberating, empowering, and creates opportunities.

1. **Face Fears Incrementally**
   Instead of avoiding fear, approach it in small, manageable doses. Each step forward reduces its grip.

   Example: If you fear vulnerability, share a personal story with a trusted friend before sharing it publicly.

2. **Surround Yourself with Supportive People**
   Authenticity flourishes in environments where you feel safe and supported. Seek relationships that honor your growth.

   Example: Join groups or communities that align with your values and goals.

3. **Embrace Imperfection**
   Growth comes through trial and error. Mistakes are not reflections of inadequacy but stepping stones to your highest potential.

   Example: Share your talents boldly, knowing that each attempt refines your abilities.

Evidence-Based Analysis: Discovering Your Core Values

Discovering your core values is critical in embracing your authentic self and achieving true freedom. Core values are an internal compass that guides decision-making, relationships, and personal fulfillment. Research in psychology, neuroscience, and behavioral sciences supports the idea that individuals who understand and live by their values experience greater well-being, resilience, and life satisfaction (Schwartz, 2012).

The Psychological Basis of Core Values

Values are deeply ingrained beliefs that shape how we perceive the world and make choices. According to **Cognitive-Behavioral Therapy (CBT)**, internalized beliefs and values influence our thoughts, emotions, and behaviors (Beck, 1976). When we align our actions with our true values, we experience coherence, meaning, and self-fulfillment. Conversely, when we live out of alignment with our values—often due to societal or familial conditioning—we experience stress, inner conflict, and dissatisfaction.

Dr. Shalom Schwartz's (1992, 2012) research on the *Theory of Basic Human Values* identifies universal values that drive human behavior, including self-direction, benevolence, and personal growth. When individuals clarify their values and prioritize them daily, they cultivate authenticity and reduce external pressures that lead to stress and self-doubt. Remind yourself of the benefits of authenticity. Being authentic makes you more confident, comfortable, and likely to have fulfilling relationships. Surround yourself with supportive people and practice self-acceptance. Stand up for yourself.

The Neuroscience of Values and Decision-Making

Neuroscientific studies reveal that values are deeply embedded in the brain's **prefrontal cortex**, which is responsible for decision-making, self-reflection, and goal-setting (Moll et al., 2005). The **limbic system**, particularly the **amygdala**, plays a role in emotional responses to value-based decisions. When individuals act against their core values, the brain registers discomfort, often leading to anxiety or cognitive dissonance (Festinger, 1957).

However, research shows that practicing **mindfulness and self-reflection** strengthens neural pathways that support values-based decision-making (Hölzel et al., 2011). By engaging in self-awareness exercises, individuals can train their brains to make choices that align with their authentic selves, reducing stress and increasing life satisfaction. Sometimes, life will teach you what you do and don't want; other times, it doesn't. Very often, people quit majors, jobs, and relationships because they lack the self-awareness to identify their own self-sabotaging behaviors. The fact that something is uncomfortable does not necessarily mean you need to quit, and most people do that because they lack self-awareness.

For example, you may think you love your current job, but when you journal about it, you find that you want to improve some aspects of your career. Another example is when you and your spouse have conversations about your financial situation, you find this stressful. However, upon further introspection, you may find that it is not about discussing finances but more about how you communicate about them.

In other words, self-awareness activities encourage you to reflect deeply on your feelings and help you become more conscious of your thoughts, reactions, and experiences. With that knowledge, you can recognize your positive traits or modify your behavior. You can take steps toward a more fulfilling career once you've identified what's not working in your role. Additionally, you can learn to alter your communication style after uncovering shortcomings in your communication with your partner.

The Impact of Core Values on Mental Health and Well-Being

A growing body of research supports the idea that individuals who actively live by their core values experience **higher levels of psychological well-being, self-confidence, and resilience** (Sheldon & Elliot, 1999). When people clarify and commit to their values, they experience:

1. **Greater Life Satisfaction:** Studies show that values-driven living increases subjective well-being and fulfillment (Sagiv & Schwartz, 2000).
2. **Reduced Stress and Anxiety:** Values alignment reduces cognitive dissonance, a psychological discomfort caused by acting against personal beliefs (Festinger, 1957).
3. **Increased Resilience:** A study by Park & Peterson (2009) found that individuals who identify and live by their strengths and values are more resilient in facing life challenges.
4. **Authentic Relationships:** Living according to core values fosters deeper, more meaningful relationships, as individuals attract like-minded people who support their true selves (Deci & Ryan, 2000).

Steps to Discovering Your Core Values

Research-backed methods to uncover personal values include **self-reflection, journaling, and guided exercises** designed to clarify priorities and authentic desires (Seligman, 2011).

Step 1: Self-Reflection and Awareness

One of the most effective ways to identify core values is through **self-reflection**. According to Acceptance and Commitment Therapy (ACT), asking deep questions helps uncover unconscious values that shape behavior (Hayes, Strosahl, & Wilson, 1999).

Questions to Consider:

- When have I felt the most fulfilled in my life?
- What qualities do I admire in others and wish to cultivate in myself?
- How would I choose to live if I had unlimited resources and time?

Step 2: Identifying Peak Experiences

Positive psychology research suggests that recalling **peak experiences**—moments when we felt the most alive and fulfilled—reveals our true values (Csikszentmihalyi, 1990).

Exercise: Write about a time when you felt deeply fulfilled. Identify the values present at that moment (e.g., creativity, connection, freedom).

Step 3: Prioritizing Values

A common challenge is distinguishing **authentic values** from those imposed by society, culture, or family expectations. Studies suggest using **values ranking exercises** to clarify priorities (Schwartz, 2012).

Activity:

- List 10-15 values that resonate with you (e.g., honesty, family, adventure, security, faith, service).
- Rank them in order of importance.

- Identify the top three values that truly define your authentic self.
- Visualize yourself having a conversation with your future self. They assure you that all of your wildest dreams have come true. What immediately comes to mind
- How does your body feel if you imagine embodying your most authentic self
- What activities does your authentic self participate in that you hold yourself back from doing now?
- What are words people have used to describe you that made you feel good and proud?
- Who are the people that you let your guard down around, and how do you show up differently around these people?

_____

_____

_____

_____

_____

Step 4: Aligning Actions with Values

According to the Self-Determination Theory (Deci & Ryan, 1985), living in alignment with values enhances intrinsic motivation and overall well-being. This means that once values are identified, they should guide daily decisions.

Action Plan:

- Set goals that reflect your top values.
- Create a **"Values Filter"**—before making major decisions, ask: "Does this align with my core values?"
- Surround yourself with people and environments that reinforce your authentic self.

The Transformation That Comes with Discovering Your Core Values

Discovering and living by your core values is **liberating** because it frees you from societal expectations and external validation. Research supports that individuals who define their own success based on personal values rather than external pressure experience **higher self-esteem, resilience, and emotional stability** (Kasser & Ryan, 1996).

In *Embracing Your Authentic Self: A Journey to True Freedom*, the theme of self-discovery aligns with the psychological and scientific principles of values-based living. The journey of peeling back layers of conditioning and uncovering one's true values is an empowering process supported by both ancient wisdom and modern research.

Conclusion: Living Authentically Through Core Values

The evidence is clear: knowing and living by your core values leads to **greater self-awareness, fulfillment, and personal freedom**. Psychological theories, neuroscientific research, and positive psychology all support the idea that when individuals embrace their authentic values, they break free from limiting beliefs and experience deeper meaning in life.

You embark on a transformative journey that fosters personal freedom, confidence, and long-term well-being by actively identifying, prioritizing, and integrating core values into daily life.

When you encounter roadblocks in your life, self-awareness activities can assist you in exploring the issue and discovering how to leverage your strengths to overcome it. Moreover, you can and should regularly practice self-reflection, even when things are going well. Ask yourself what's working and acknowledge the value of the positive aspects of your life. You'll improve emotional and decision-making skills—fostering a lifestyle and interactions that align with your desires and needs.

Practical Exercises to Overcome Fear and Self-Doubt

Thought Journaling

Write down recurring fears or doubts. Challenge their validity and replace them with affirming statements. Try to understand where the thought comes from and whether it is related to a specific trigger or situation. In your thought journaling, question the validity of the thought. Is it based on misinterpretation or exaggeration? Try to see the situation from a different perspective or find a more positive or neutral way to interpret the thought.

_____

_____

_____

_____

_____

_____

_____

_____

Daily Affirmations

Create statements of self-belief, such as "I am capable of achieving great things." Repeat them regularly to reprogram your subconscious.

Visualization

Close your eyes and vividly imagine yourself succeeding in a situation you fear. Feel the emotions of confidence, joy, and accomplishment.

Reframe Specific Fears

- Fear: "I'm not capable of leading a team."
- Impact: "I avoid leadership roles, holding back my career."
- Reframe: "Leadership is a skill I can develop with practice and learning."

Mindfulness Practice for Inner Strength

Find a quiet space and focus on your breath. With each exhale, release fear; with each inhale, welcome courage. Silently affirm:

- "I release doubt and embrace my potential."
- "I am strong, capable, and enough."

Key Takeaway

Fear and self-doubt are not obstacles to avoid but rather opportunities for growth. You align with your most authentic self by reframing limiting beliefs, nurturing confidence, and taking courageous steps. This alignment fosters a life of fulfillment, purpose and joy.

Chapter 5

Breaking Free from People-Pleasing

Are you a people-pleaser? A people-pleaser craves validation and reassurance and is afraid to disappoint others because they worry about rejection or abandonment. They may go to great lengths to help others, even when not asked, and they often take the blame for things that were not their fault.

Deep within the human heart lies a longing for acceptance. We yearn to hear words of approval, to feel the warmth of acknowledgment, and to secure our place in the hearts of others. Yet, when this desire dominates, it can lead us down the path of people-pleasing, where we sacrifice our well-being to satisfy others.

The Apostle Paul posed a question that challenges us to examine this tendency: *"Am I now trying to win the approval of human beings, or of God? If I were still trying to please people, I would not be a servant of Christ"* (Galatians 1:10). These words illuminate a higher truth: true freedom is found not in the praise of men but in aligning ourselves with divine purpose.

The Roots of People-Pleasing

Many of us develop people-pleasing behaviors early in life. Perhaps you learned that being agreeable earned you affection or that avoiding conflict kept you safe. Although these patterns were initially protective, they often become burdensome in adulthood.

Reflect on these common roots:

1. **The Desire for Approval**: *"For they loved human praise more than praise from God"* (John 12:43). In seeking validation from others, we may forget that the love of the Divine is unconditional and eternal.
2. **Fear of Rejection**: Fear whispers that saying "no" will lead to loss, but Scripture reminds us, *"The Lord is my helper; I will not be afraid. What can mere mortals do to me?"* (Hebrews 13:6).
3. **Conditional Love**: If you've been taught that love must be earned, know that God's love is not conditional. *"I have loved you with an everlasting love; I have drawn you with unfailing kindness"* (Jeremiah 31:3).

Though these behaviors served a purpose, they often led to exhaustion, resentment, and a diminished sense of self. But take heart—you can break free.

Reclaiming Your Authentic Self

Breaking free from people-pleasing is not a selfish act; it is an act of self-respect and alignment with your divine calling. Jesus taught us the balance between serving others and honoring our needs when He said, *"Come to me, all you who are weary and burdened, and I will give you rest"* (Matthew 11:28).

Let us explore practical steps to embrace this transformation:

1. Cultivate Self-Awareness

Recognize the moments when you're tempted to please others at your own expense. Pause and ask yourself:

- *Am I seeking approval from others or following my inner guidance?*
- *Does this align with my values and priorities?*

Remember the wisdom of Proverbs 4:23: *"Above all else, guard your heart, for everything you do flows from it."*

2. Set Healthy Boundaries

Boundaries are a sacred act of self-care. They honor your time and energy while maintaining respect for others. When Jesus often withdrew to solitary places to pray (Luke 5:16), He demonstrated the importance of setting boundaries to recharge spiritually. Practice saying no with grace:

"Thank you for understanding, but I need to focus on other commitments right now."

3. Replace Fear with Faith

Fear is a barrier, but faith is the bridge to freedom. *"God has not given us a spirit of fear, but of power and of love and of a sound mind"* (2 Timothy 1:7). When fear arises, anchor yourself in this truth and affirm, "I act from love and authenticity, not fear."

4. Affirm Your Worth

Your value is inherent, not earned through deeds or the approval of others. Reflect on this powerful affirmation: *"I praise you because I am fearfully and wonderfully made"* (Psalm 139:14). Speak this truth over yourself until it becomes a living reality.

Exercises to Strengthen Your Journey

1. **Reflective Journaling:** Write about moments when you felt compelled to please others. How did it feel? How could

you respond differently next time? Recognize when you're prioritizing others' needs and desires over your own. Consider what situations trigger these behaviors and what needs they are trying to fulfill. Clearly define your limits and communicate them to others. This might involve saying no to requests, setting time limits for interactions, or establishing limits on what you're willing to do.

_____

_____

_____

_____

_____

2. **Role-Playing Assertiveness** Practice expressing your needs in a safe environment. Start with a trusted friend and imagine how Jesus gently yet firmly communicated His mission.
3. **Mindful Prayer** Before making a decision, pause to pray: _"Lord, guide me to act in alignment with Your will. Help me honor both You and the gifts You've placed within me."_

Key Takeaway

Jesus' life was a perfect balance of service and self-care. By following His example and embracing your God-given worth, you can break free from people-pleasing and live a life of authenticity and purpose. As Paul reminds us, _"It is for freedom that Christ has set us free"_ (Galatians 5:1). You can step into that freedom today.

I know that breaking free from people-pleasing can feel daunting. You might worry about how others will react or whether your relationships will crumble when you start saying no more often.

However, consider all the energy you have poured into making others happy, often at the expense of your well-being. Imagine redirecting that same energy toward growing yourself, cultivating healthier relationships, and experiencing true emotional freedom. Sounds life-changing, right?

As you embark on this journey, remember that the insights and strategies shared in this book are here to support you every step of the way. You have the tools to break free from people-pleasing in your relationships and work, set healthy boundaries, and build self-esteem. And the best part? You'll be doing it all while staying true to who you are.

So, take a deep breath and get ready to embrace the authentic, empowered version of yourself that's been waiting to show up. The road ahead might be challenging, but the rewards are genuinely life changing. You've got this, and I'm cheering you on every step of the way.

Chapter 6

The Power of
Self-Compassion

In the rush of daily life, we often extend kindness and understanding to others but forget to offer the same to ourselves. Self-compassion—the art of treating yourself with the same kindness, care, and forgiveness you'd show a dear friend—is transformative. It allows you to confront self-criticism, embrace your humanity, and create space for growth and authenticity. As Psalm 34:18 reminds us, "The Lord is close to the broken-hearted and saves those who are crushed in spirit." This truth encourages us to offer ourselves the same grace we would seek from God during difficult times.

This chapter delves into the concept of self-compassion, explores the toll of self-criticism, and offers practical strategies to nurture a kinder relationship with yourself. By the end, you'll see self-compassion not as a luxury but as a necessity for living authentically and fully. It involves recognizing shared humanity, acknowledging mistakes, and approaching challenges with a compassionate mindset.

Self-compassion, essentially giving yourself a bit of grace, can be very useful when feeling overwhelmed. It allows us to accept that we're not perfect and that we're not going to do everything flawlessly. This mindset enables us to appreciate how much we accomplish, despite how challenging it may seem.

Self-compassion involves making a U-turn and offering yourself the same kindness you would naturally extend to a friend when you are the one who is struggling or feeling bad about yourself. It means being supportive when facing challenges, feeling inadequate, or making mistakes. Instead of simply ignoring the pain with a 'stiff upper lip' mentality or being overwhelmed by negative thoughts and emotions, you can pause and tell yourself, "This is difficult right now. How can I comfort and care for myself in this situation? "

Recognizing Self-Criticism

Self-criticism often disguises itself as motivation, whispering that relentless pressure is the only way to succeed. However, it does more harm than good, eroding self-esteem and hindering growth. Believe it or not, it's evolved for the best of intentions. It wants to protect us and keep us safe in the world, but it does so by shaming and picking at us.

You can push yourself pretty far by beating yourself up to take action, but you can't reach your desired destination in life or feel the way you want. Whenever you achieve your goal, you will arrive feeling exhausted, stressed, and barely hanging on because your inner critic will continuously raise the bar

You will only feel the way you desire and achieve what you want in your work life when you can manage your thoughts and act on what your body tells you about your desires. Try celebrating each small victory. Begin training your brain to focus on what you are doing well.

Personal Reflection

For years, I believed that holding myself to impossibly high standards was the path to success. Each mistake triggered a harsh inner dialogue, leaving me feeling inadequate and unworthy. Perfectionism is a trait that turns life into an endless report card on accomplishments or appearances. When healthy, it can be self-motivating and drive you to overcome adversity and achieve success. However, when unhealthy, it can lead to a fast and enduring track to unhappiness.

What makes extreme perfectionism so toxic is that while those in its grip desire success, they focus more on avoiding failure, which results in a negative orientation. They don't believe in unconditional love and expect others' affection and approval to depend on flawless performance.

Example: After delivering a work presentation, I fixated on minor errors, replaying them in my mind and chastising myself for not being perfect. My focus on imperfections overshadowed the overall success of the presentation.

Key Insight

Self-criticism creates a cycle of negativity. The more you berate yourself, the harder it becomes to see your strengths and achievements. Isaiah 43:1 provides a comforting counterpoint: "Do not fear, for I have redeemed you; I have summoned you by name; you are mine." Knowing we are valued and cherished can help break the cycle of harsh self-judgment.

Though we may have high standards, it is important to view ourselves through loving eyes. Berating ourselves only makes our spirit sink. Self-improvement comes from a loving mindset.

Cultivating Self-Compassion

The turning point came when I realized that the key to resilience and growth was not criticism but compassion. I began treating myself with the same kindness I extended to others. In today's fast-paced world filled with pressures and constant comparisons, embracing self-compassion is a powerful tool for personal growth and well-being. This practice encourages us to extend to ourselves the same gentleness, empathy, and encouragement that we readily offer to our beloved friends, especially during difficult times. By nurturing self-compassion, we not only strengthen our resilience but also enhance our self-esteem, preparing us to navigate life's complexities with greater confidence and poise.

Here are the strategies that helped me develop self-compassion:

Mindful Awareness

Pay attention to your inner dialogue. Notice when self-criticism arises and observe it without judgment. We all have an inner critic, but you don't have to agree with everything it says. There are ways to work with and even challenge or defy this automatic voice in your head. Be aware of moments when you feel overwhelmed by negativity or self-doubt. It may surface when you make a mistake, face a challenge, or feel uncomfortable.

Example: During moments of self-doubt, I paused to acknowledge my feelings, saying, "I see that you're struggling right now, and that's okay." This simple act of mindfulness created space for self-kindness.

Reframing Negative Thoughts

Challenge your inner critic by reframing harsh thoughts into supportive ones. The first step in interrupting this pattern is to notice when it is happening rather than letting it go unchecked like usual. When you hear the inner critic pipe up, have one of those show-stopping scratch-the-record moments and pay close attention to what was said.

Example: Instead of thinking, "I always mess things up," I reframed it as, "Everyone makes mistakes; this is an opportunity to learn and grow." Over time, this shift helped me build a more compassionate inner voice.

Writing Self-Compassion Letters

Write letters to yourself, addressing your struggles with empathy and understanding. This powerful practice invites self-reflection, goal-setting, and personal growth. It allows you to capture the essence of who you are today and provides a glimpse into the person you aspire to become. When you have finished writing your letter, read it back to yourself out loud in a warm, caring voice. Take your time with this to allow your mind to hear and feel the words, feelings, and intentions behind the letter.

Example: In one letter, I acknowledged my feelings of inadequacy after a professional setback, reminding myself that it's human to face difficulties. I offered words of encouragement, just as I would to a dear friend.

Practicing Self-Kindness

Make a conscious effort to engage in activities that nurture your well-being and bring you joy. Participating in joyful activities can significantly enhance your overall well-being. Research shows that when activities align with our personal interests, goals, values, and personality traits, they are likely to yield higher levels of satisfaction. Simple pleasures, such as feeling the sun on your face or enjoying a freshly made bed, can uplift your mood. Moreover, creative outlets like writing letters, cooking, and mixing cocktails offer both satisfaction and fulfillment joy.

Spending quality time with friends and family fosters emotional connections, which are essential for happiness. Activities such as shared game nights or outdoor adventures with loved ones cultivate experiences that anchor joy memories.

Incorporating a variety of these small yet meaningful activities into your daily routine can help foster a lasting sense of joy in your life. Whether it's enjoying moments of laughter, engaging in hobbies that spark your interest, or being mindful of the little pleasures found in everyday activities, the pursuit of joy remains personal and adaptable to your own lifestyle. Keeping track of these activities and regularly evaluating their impact on your satisfaction can further enhance your journey toward happiness.

Example: I allowed myself to take breaks when needed, indulged in hobbies like painting and gardening, and spoke to myself with gentle affirmations.

Seeking Support

Share your journey with trusted friends, mentors, or therapists who can provide perspective and encouragement. When you're having a tough day, sometimes talking to a good friend is all it takes to help turn things around. Having someone to listen and give you the "you got this" pep talk can assist you in working through struggles and feeling more empowered to face life's curveballs. Study after study supports this—when we feel connected and supported, we're more resilient, less stressed, and healthier.

Social support is often identified as a key component of solid relationships and strong psychological health, but what exactly does it mean? Social support involves having a network of family and friends you can turn to in times of need. Whether you are facing a personal crisis and need immediate assistance, or you want to spend time with people who care about you, these relationships play a critical role in how you function in your day-to-day life. Such connections offer practical support (think showing up with a homemade meal when you're feeling sick), good advice, emotional validation, and a comforting shoulder to cry on.

Example: Discussing my experiences with a close friend reminded me that I wasn't alone in facing challenges, and their support reinforced my commitment to self-kindness.

The Impact of Self-Compassion

We all tend to blame ourselves when things go wrong in life. Self-compassion is the antidote. It is the capacity to be kind to ourselves during times of suffering or feelings of inadequacy. Instead of shutting down, behaving unkindly, or engaging in other harmful patterns, we can rise above our pain and embrace the wonderfully human aspects of our existence.

Embracing self-compassion has created profound shifts in my life:

- **Reduced Self-Criticism:** I no longer berate myself for imperfections but accept them as part of being human.
- **Enhanced Resilience:** Self-compassion has equipped me to navigate challenges with greater ease and adaptability.
- **Improved Relationships:** Being kinder to myself has made me more empathetic and understanding toward others.
- **Increased Authenticity:** Self-compassion has empowered me to live more authentically, free from fear of judgment.

We all encounter seemingly unbearable situations at times. Chances are, you have already experienced this. It's simply part of the human condition. That's when the miracle of self-compassion comes to the rescue: helping us face our inevitable crises and transform our experience through mindful awareness, a sense of common humanity, and self-kindness.

Practical Exercises for Cultivating Self-Compassion

1. **Self-Compassion Journal:** Maintain a journal to reflect on moments of self-criticism. For each instance:
   - Write down the negative thought.
   - Challenge its validity.
   - Reframe it with a compassionate response.
   Example:
      i. Negative Thought: "I failed that presentation."
      ii. Reframe: "I did my best, and I can learn from this experience to improve next time."

To cultivate self-compassion, practice mindfulness, kindness, and recognize common humanity. Shift your perspective, writing compassionate letters to yourself, and engaging in self-care activities are also beneficial. Remember to replace negative self-talk with positive affirmations and celebrate small victories.

_____

_____

_____

_____

_____

2. **Guided Meditations:** Engage in self-compassion meditations to foster a sense of kindness toward yourself.
   - **Visualization:** Imagine yourself as a child and offer the compassion you needed in that moment.
   - **Loving-Kindness:** Silently repeat phrases like, "May I be kind to myself. May I be at peace."

3. **Affirmations** Develop a set of self-compassionate affirmations to recite daily:
   - "I am doing the best I can with the resources I have."
   - "I deserve love and kindness, especially from myself."

4. **Write a Self-Compassion Letter:** Write a letter to yourself, addressing your struggles with empathy and support. Use this letter to remind yourself of your strengths and resilience.

Exercise for Reflection

Write a letter to yourself:

- Begin by acknowledging a recent struggle or challenge.
- Offer comfort and encouragement to yourself as you would to a dear friend.
- Conclude with a reminder that you are worthy of love and kindness, even in the most challenging times.

Showing kindness and love to yourself, also known as self-compassion, is crucial for your overall well-being and mental health. It involves treating yourself with the same care, understanding, and support you would offer a friend, especially during challenging times. This practice can reduce negative self-talk, increase resilience, and foster a more positive outlook on life.

Self-compassion helps lower the intensity of negative emotions like anxiety and depression by fostering a sense of inner peace and security. When you're kind to yourself, you're better equipped to bounce back from setbacks and adversity, developing a greater capacity to cope with difficult situations. Self-compassion allows you to acknowledge your worth, love yourself unconditionally, and approach challenges with a more positive mindset.

By practicing self-compassion, you can quiet the inner critic and replace negative self-talk with more supportive and encouraging thoughts. Research indicates that self-compassion can have a beneficial effect on the immune system. Being kind to yourself can help reduce stress levels, which can contribute to lower blood pressure.

_____

_____

_____

_____

_____

_____

_____

_____

_____

_____

_____

_____

_____

_____

_____

Mindfulness Integration

Practice a loving-kindness meditation:

- Sit in a comfortable position and close your eyes.
- Take three deep breaths to center yourself.

Silently repeat the following phrases:

- "May I be kind to myself."
- "May I forgive myself."
- "May I embrace my imperfections."

Gradually extend these wishes to others, fostering a sense of connection and compassion.

Key Takeaway

Self-compassion is crucial for resilience, self-acceptance, and authenticity. You pave the way for a more fulfilling and authentic life by treating yourself with kindness, understanding, and forgiveness. Self-compassion reduces stress and anxiety by encouraging a kind and understanding attitude towards oneself. This practice promotes emotional resilience, decreases self-criticism, and fosters a balanced perspective on life's challenges, ultimately enhancing mental well-being and lowering stress levels.

Most importantly, having compassion for yourself means honoring and accepting your humanity. Things will not always go your way. You will encounter frustrating times, experience loss, make mistakes, fall short of your ideals, and face your limitations. This is part of being human, a reality shared by all of us. The more open you are to this reality and work with it instead of constantly fighting against it, the more you will be able to feel compassion for yourself and your fellow humans in the journey of life.

Part 3
Cultivating Self-Awareness and Embracing Vulnerability

Chapter 7

The Power of Self-Awareness

Self-awareness is the cornerstone of authentic living. It allows us to step off autopilot and observe our thoughts, emotions, and behaviors with curiosity rather than judgment. This understanding equips us to make intentional choices that align with our values, nurture our well-being, and strengthen our connections with others. Proverbs 27:19 reminds us, "As water reflects the face, so one's life reflects the heart." Understanding our inner world can better align our actions with our true selves.

In this chapter, we'll explore the transformative journey of developing self-awareness. Drawing from my personal experiences and practical techniques, I invite you to embark on a path toward deeper self-understanding and alignment with your true self.

Understanding Self-Awareness

Self-awareness is the ability to consciously recognize and understand your inner world—your thoughts, feelings, and actions—and how they influence your life. It involves observing patterns, identifying triggers, and understanding the motivations behind your decisions. As James 1:23-25 illustrates, self-awareness is like looking into a mirror.

We can go about our day without giving our inner self any extra thought, merely thinking, feeling, and acting as we will; however, we can also focus our attention on that inner self. When we engage in self-awareness, we can give some thought to whether we are thinking and feeling and acting as we "should" or following our standards and values. This is known as comparing to our standards of correctness. We engage in this daily, utilizing these standards to assess the rightness of our thoughts and actions. Applying these standards is a crucial aspect of practicing self-control as we evaluate and decide if we are making the right choices to reach our goals.

When we examine ourselves honestly but fail to act on that awareness, we miss opportunities for growth and transformation. Listening and responding to our inner reflections fosters meaningful change.

Why Self-Awareness Matters

- It helps you identify behaviors and beliefs that no longer serve you.
- It fosters better emotional regulation and decision-making.
- It paves the way for personal growth and meaningful relationships.

Key Insight

Self-awareness is not about perfection. It's about understanding yourself with compassion and using that understanding to make choices that align with your authentic self.

My Journey to Self-Awareness

For much of my life, I reacted to situations on autopilot, unaware of the habitual thoughts and emotions driving my behavior. This lack of awareness led to decisions that often conflicted with my values, leaving me disconnected and dissatisfied.

Example: I often overcommitted to social engagements, overlooking my need for rest. This tendency to prioritize others over myself led to burnout and resentment, yet I continued the cycle because I wasn't attuned to the internal cues indicating my need for balance. It wasn't until I began developing self-awareness that I recognized and broke free from this pattern.

Techniques for Enhancing Self-Awareness

Self-awareness is the ability to see yourself clearly and objectively through reflection and introspection. Although achieving total objectivity about oneself may be impossible (this debate has persisted throughout the history of philosophy), there are undoubtedly degrees of self-awareness. It exists on a spectrum.

Although everyone has a fundamental idea of self-awareness, we don't know exactly where it comes from, what its precursors are, or why some people seem to have more or less than others. The following techniques can give you some potential answers to these questions.

Mindful Observation

Mindfulness is the practice of observing your thoughts, feelings, and behaviors without judgment. It helps you stay present and notice internal experiences as they unfold. This can help you become more aware of your internal state and your reactions to things. Mindfulness can also help you identify your thoughts and feelings and avoid getting so caught up in them that you lose your hold on your "self."

Example: During a disagreement, I noticed feelings of defensiveness rising. Instead of reacting impulsively, I paused to observe the emotion. This pause allowed me to respond thoughtfully rather than escalating the conflict.

Body Scan Meditation

Emotions often manifest in the body before they reach conscious awareness. A body scan meditation helps you connect with these physical sensations, offering valuable insights into your emotional state. That is what I love about Yoga. While yoga is a physical practice, it is just as much a mental practice. While your body is stretching and bending and flexing, your mind is learning self-acceptance, discipline, and awareness. You become more aware of your body and all the feelings that manifest, and you become more aware of your mind and the thoughts that crop up.

Example: I noticed that anxiety often presented as tightness in my chest. Recognizing this sensation early enabled me to address the underlying emotion before it escalated.

Journaling

Writing about your thoughts and experiences is a powerful tool for self-reflection. Journaling helps you identify patterns, clarify your emotions, and gain deeper insights into your inner world.

It helps you discover what you want, what you value, and what works for you. It can also help you find out what you don't want, what is unimportant to you, and what doesn't work for you. Both aspects are equally important to learn. Whether you prefer to write free-flowing entries, bulleted lists, or poems, recording your thoughts and feelings enhances your awareness and intention.

Example: Reviewing my journal entries, I discovered a tendency to self-criticize after receiving feedback. This awareness helped me shift my perspective, approaching feedback as an opportunity for growth rather than a personal failure.

Seeking Feedback

Sometimes, others can see what we cannot. Seeking input from trusted friends, mentors, or colleagues can provide valuable perspectives and highlight blind spots. It's vital to feel we know ourselves from the inside, but external feedback helps too. Have your family and close friends describe you, and see what resonates with you and what surprises you.

Carefully consider what they say and think about it when you journal or otherwise reflect. Of course, don't take any one person's word as gospel; you need to talk to a variety of people to get a comprehensive view of yourself. And remember that at the end of the day, it's your feelings and self-beliefs that matter the most to you.

Example: A friend pointed out that I often apologized excessively, even when it was unnecessary. This feedback made me realize I lacked self-confidence in certain situations, prompting me to work on assertiveness.

Regular Mindfulness Practices

Engage in daily mindfulness exercises such as meditation, mindful breathing, or yoga. These practices train your mind to remain present, enhancing your ability to observe your thoughts and feelings without judgment.

Reflecting can be done in various ways, such as journaling, and is customizable to you. The important thing is to review your thoughts, feelings, and behaviors to see where you met your standards, where you fell short, and where you could improve

You can also reflect on your standards to see if they are good ones to hold yourself to. You can try writing in a journal, talking out loud, or simply sitting quietly and breathing as you think - whatever helps you to reflect on yourself.

Example: During stressful moments, practicing mindful breathing helped me remain calm and centered, enabling me to respond thoughtfully rather than react impulsively.

The Impact of Self-Awareness

Developing self-awareness has brought profound changes to my life:

* **Improved Decision-Making:** With a clearer understanding of my values and motivations, I now make choices that align with my authentic self.
* **Enhanced Emotional Regulation:** Recognizing my triggers has helped me manage my reactions more effectively, leading to healthier interactions.
* **Greater Self-Acceptance:** Observing myself without judgment has fostered compassion and acceptance toward my imperfections.
* **Authentic Relationships:** As I understand myself better, I engage in relationships more openly and honestly, strengthening my connections with others.

Practical Exercises for Developing Self-Awareness

Mindfulness Meditation

Set aside 10 minutes each day to sit quietly. Focus on your breath and observe your thoughts as they come and go without judgment.

Notice patterns: Do specific thoughts or feelings frequently arise? What triggers them?

Emotional Check-Ins:

Pause throughout the day to assess your emotional state. Ask yourself:

- What am I feeling right now?
- What triggered this emotion?
- How can I respond in alignment with my values?

Reflective Journaling

Write about your daily experiences, focusing on recurring themes or reactions. A reflective journal is a powerful tool for personal and professional growth, fostering self-awareness, critical thinking, and better decision-making. It helps individuals analyze their experiences, learn from them, and recognize areas for improvement. Reflective journaling promotes introspection, enabling individuals to understand their thoughts, feelings, and behaviors in various situations. By examining reactions to events and interactions, individuals can identify patterns, triggers, and areas for growth.

Reflecting on experiences and analyzing them critically boosts critical thinking skills. This involves assessing information, questioning assumptions, and forming more informed perspectives. Reflective journals offer a space to process learning experiences, identify key insights, and connect theory with practice. By examining what has been learned and how it can be applied, individuals can deepen their understanding and improve their performance in different settings.

Reflecting on past decisions and their consequences can help you make better choices in the future. By understanding what influenced previous decisions, you can develop more effective strategies and avoid repeating the same mistakes. Reflective journaling can help individuals clarify their goals, track progress, and identify the steps needed to achieve them.

Prompt: What situations brought me joy or frustration today? What did I learn about myself?

Body Awareness Practices

Engage in yoga, tai chi, or other practices that connect the mind and body. These activities heighten your awareness of how emotions manifest physically.

Exercise: Weekly Journal Practice

Keep a journal for one week, noting your thoughts and feelings at different times of the day. Look for recurring patterns or themes.

Example:

- **Observation:** I frequently feel anxious before social situations.
- **Insight:** This anxiety stems from a fear of judgment.
- **Action:** Practice affirmations to boost confidence and focus on being present in conversations.

Mindfulness Integration

Practice daily mindfulness meditation with a focus on non-judgmental observation. A guided body scan meditation can help you connect with your emotions and physical sensations, offering deeper self-awareness.

Key Takeaway

Self-awareness is the foundation of authentic living. Observing yourself with curiosity and compassion allows you to identify patterns, make intentional choices, and align your life with your true self. As we embrace the wisdom of Proverbs and James, we're reminded that self-awareness reflects the heart and guides us to live in alignment with our deepest values.

The connection between meditation, mindfulness, and self-awareness is clear, so it's no surprise that practicing the first two will naturally lead to more of the third.

When we meditate or practice mindfulness, we pay attention to the aspects that often get overlooked in our busy day-to-day lives: the present moment and our internal experiences. Those who understand their thought processes and patterns can better adapt and improve them, by being aware of these processes and patterns and by providing themselves with a mechanism for practice and enhancement.

Chapter 8

Embracing Vulnerability

Vulnerability is the gateway to authentic living. It is not a sign of weakness but a profound strength, a divine invitation to allow your true self to shine through without pretence. To be vulnerable is to trust that in your imperfections, grace abounds. As the Apostle Paul reminds us, "My grace is sufficient for you, for my power is made perfect in weakness" (2 Corinthians 12:9).

In this chapter, we explore how vulnerability deepens relationships, nurtures trust, and strengthens authenticity, all while emphasizing the wisdom of maintaining healthy boundaries. True vulnerability is not about exposing yourself recklessly; it is about aligning your openness with your values and fostering genuine connections.

Recognizing Vulnerability as Strength

For years, I misunderstood vulnerability as a liability. I believed strength meant maintaining a facade of composure, always having the answers, and never revealing insecurity. But this belief kept me from experiencing the transformative power of authenticity.

When I finally allowed myself to be seen as I truly was, something remarkable happened: I grew stronger. I learned that vulnerability is not about weakness but about courage—the courage to trust in divine grace and show up as your authentic self. Your authentic self is who you really are deep down. The part of you that doesn't care what others think. Learning how to be your authentic self is an essential part of building meaningful relationships. Authenticity happens when your words, actions, and behaviors consistently match your core identity.

A Shift in Perspective

I discovered that vulnerability shared with discernment fosters trust and growth. In a professional setting, I once hesitated to admit I had no answer, fearing it would undermine my credibility. However, when I chose honesty, acknowledged my limitations, and invited my team's input, it strengthened our collaboration and mutual respect. Authenticity inspires connection far more than the illusion of perfection.

Sharing Imperfections to Foster Connection

Hiding our imperfections isolates us. Sharing them, however, creates spaces where others feel safe to do the same. Vulnerability becomes the bridge to connection, allowing us to see and be seen in our humanity.

When I shared my struggles with anxiety with a close friend, it opened the door to a deeply healing conversation. We both felt a profound sense of mutual support. Vulnerability, when shared thoughtfully, invites others into a sacred space of trust and empathy, reflecting the eternal truth that "neither death nor life... nor anything else in all creation... will be able to separate us from the love of God" (Romans 8:38–39).

Maintaining Healthy Boundaries

To embrace vulnerability wisely, we must pair it with discernment. Sharing your true self does not mean abandoning discretion. It is about choosing the proper context and audience for your openness. Vulnerability is not about exposing yourself to unnecessary pain or letting go of boundaries; it's about being brave enough to show up in the world as your authentic self. When you embrace vulnerability, you stop pretending to be someone you're not, unlocking a deeper sense of self-worth and inner strength.

True strength doesn't come from hiding our emotions or pretending everything is fine. It comes from the courage to be vulnerable, to admit when we need help, and to trust that we are enough—even in our imperfections.

The next time you feel the urge to don your emotional armor, remember vulnerability is your superpower. It serves as the gateway to connection, growth, and true strength. Embrace it and observe how it transforms your life.

How to Share Vulnerably and Safely

- **Discern Your Audience:** Not everyone deserves access to your inner world. Share with those who have earned your trust.
- **Gradual Openness:** Begin with small disclosures, allowing trust to grow naturally.
- **Reflect on Intentions:** Ask yourself why you're sharing. Are you seeking connection and authenticity, or are you looking for external validation?
- When I entered a new relationship, I shared my personal experiences gradually, building trust over time. This approach created a foundation of mutual respect and understanding, ensuring that my vulnerability was met with care.

Practical Steps to Embrace Vulnerability

Acknowledge Your Fears - Fear often accompanies vulnerability. Ask yourself:

- What am I afraid of—judgment, rejection, or failure?
- How can I confront this fear with faith and trust?
- **Action Step:** Write down your fears and affirm your trust in God's grace to guide you through them.

Start Small

- Begin practicing vulnerability in low-risk settings.
- Share a minor insecurity with someone you trust and observe their response.
- Notice the freedom that comes from authenticity.

Seek Support

- Surround yourself with empathetic individuals who value authenticity. They will remind you that vulnerability is a strength.
- Join a supportive group
- Confide in a trusted mentor who can encourage you.

Reflect on Experiences

- After being vulnerable, take time to reflect:
- How did it feel to share?
- What did you learn about yourself and your relationships?

The Impact of Vulnerability

Embracing vulnerability has transformed my life in ways I never imagined:

- **Deeper Relationships:** Authenticity has strengthened my bonds with others, fostering trust and mutual understanding.
- **Greater Self-Acceptance:** Sharing my imperfections has allowed me to embrace them, freeing me from shame or fear of judgment.

- **Increased Resilience:** Vulnerability has equipped me to face challenges with courage, knowing that I am supported by divine love and grace.

Practical Exercises

1. **Identify Areas for Growth**
   Choose one area where you tend to avoid vulnerability. Write down why you resist and take one small step toward openness.

   Example: If you hesitate to share feelings with your partner, start by expressing a positive emotion like gratitude or excitement. Sharing your feelings helps build a bond that not only improves your relationship but can also increase closeness in everyday life, regardless of what is happening in your world.

   _____

   _____

   _____

   _____

2. **Practice Mindful Self-Compassion**
   Embrace the discomfort of vulnerability with kindness. Repeat affirmations that remind you of your inner strength:

   - "I am safe to express my true self."
   - "My vulnerability is a reflection of divine strength."

3. **Loving-Kindness Meditation**
   Meditate on compassion for yourself and others:

- Sit quietly and breathe deeply.
- Silently repeat phrases like, "May I accept myself as I am," and, "May I extend love and understanding to others."

Key Takeaway

Vulnerability is a divine strength that enriches every aspect of life. It fosters deeper connections, cultivates self-acceptance, and empowers authentic living. When guided by faith and paired with healthy boundaries, vulnerability becomes a source of profound growth and intimacy, reflecting God's perfect love. This is why God's love is so transformative. It doesn't stop at accepting us; it empowers us.

As Romans 5:8 says: "But God demonstrates His love toward us, in that while we were still sinners, Christ died for us." While we were at our worst, God loved us at His best. This kind of love removes the fear of inadequacy and replaces it with the confidence to become. The key is surrendering to God's perfect love. When we do, we stop striving to prove ourselves and start thriving in the assurance that we're already accepted.

In a world where love often comes with conditions, God's perfect love stands apart. It accepts us as we are, empowers us to become, and transforms vulnerability into a source of strength. As you reflect on this, remember the words of Jesus in Matthew 11:28-30: "Come to Me, all you who labor and are heavy laden, and I will give you rest. Take My yoke upon you and learn from Me, for I am gentle and lowly in heart, and you will find rest for your souls. For My yoke is easy, and My burden is light."

When we rest in His love, we find the freedom to live without fear, thrive without striving, and embrace vulnerability as the starting point for extraordinary transformation.

Chapter 9

The Art of Self-Expression

Self-expression is the divine bridge between your inner essence and the world around you. It is your sacred way of revealing the thoughts, emotions, and gifts uniquely given to you by the Creator. Authentic self-expression illuminates your inner truth and fosters deeper connection, understanding, and fulfillment in your life.

As Ephesians 2:10 reminds us, "For we are God's handiwork, created in Christ Jesus to do good works, which God prepared in advance for us to do." You are crafted with intention, and the creative ways you express yourself are part of that greater design. Let us now explore how embracing self-expression leads you closer to your authentic self and the fulfillment of your divine purpose.

Art as a Mirror to the Soul

Art is one of the most profound ways to reveal the soul's depths. It bypasses the limitations of words, allowing emotions and spiritual insights to flow freely into the physical realm. When you express yourself through art, you align with the Spirit within, creating a tangible reflection of your inner world.

Example: During a challenging period of my life, I was drawn to painting as a way to release my emotions. Without formal training, I let my intuition guide the brush, and what emerged on the canvas was a vivid portrayal of my struggles and victories. Through this process, I felt a sense of peace, as though my spirit was whispering, "Cast all your anxieties on Him, for He cares for you" (1 Peter 5:7).

Practical Tip: Engage with visual art, whether through drawing, painting, or sculpting. Focus on the process, not perfection, and allow the Spirit to guide your expression.

Writing as a Path to Self-Discovery

Writing is a sacred tool for reflection and discovery, allowing you to articulate your heart's and spirit's whispers. Journaling or storytelling transforms scattered thoughts into clarity, grounding you in truth.

Example: Each morning, I journaled my thoughts and feelings, allowing my spirit to commune with the divine wisdom within me. I found myself uncovering desires and fears that had been buried, gaining a deeper understanding of God's purpose for my life. As 1 Peter 4:10 encourages, "Each of you should use whatever gift you have received to serve others." Writing became a gift that served my growth and connection with others.

Practical Tip: Start journaling each day with prompts such as:

- What am I grateful for today?
- What message does my heart wish to express?
- Is there something I need to forgive myself or others for?
- What energizes me and what drains me?

The practice of reflective journaling provides many benefits, including increasing self-awareness and supporting personal growth. By taking time to explore your thoughts, feelings, and experiences, you build a stronger connection with your inner self and gain a clearer understanding of your life's path.

_____

_____

_____

_____

_____

_____

_____

Focusing on my self-growth has allowed me to develop a self-made sense of propriety and respectability. A great deal of progress can be achieved through conversations with oneself, answering questions that delve deeper into the various aspects that shape who we are. Keeping a physical form of my internal conversations through journaling allows me to track my progress. I encourage you to do the same, as writing down your thoughts is invaluable for understanding what makes you tick and the changes you can make, to see where you are headed.

Music as an Emotional Outlet

Music carries a divine frequency that touches the soul in ways words cannot. Whether you listen, play, or compose, music provides a channel for emotional release and connection.

Example: When I learned to play the guitar, I often composed melodies that spoke to my soul's unspoken prayers. Each note echoed Psalm 100:1: "Make a joyful noise to the Lord, all the earth!"

Sharing these melodies with friends created bonds of empathy and joy.

Practical Tip: Create a playlist that resonates with your emotions or explore playing a simple instrument. Let the music become your prayer and your joy.

Dance as a Celebration of Authenticity

Movement is a celebration of life and divine authenticity. Dance allows you to connect with your body and spirit, expressing joy, sorrow, and every emotion in between through the sacred rhythm of motion.

Example: When I joined a dance class, I was reminded of the freedom of childlike faith. I let go of self-consciousness and allowed my body to rejoice in its God-given grace. This experience brought to life the words of Psalm 149:3: "Let them praise His name with dancing."

Practical Tip: Find a form of dance or movement that speaks to your spirit. Move with the intention of expressing gratitude for the life within you.

Daily Conversations as Opportunities for Authenticity

Authentic self-expression isn't confined to the arts; it manifests in everyday interactions. When you speak your truth with love, you create opportunities for connection and understanding.

Example: I found a sense of freedom and deeper relationships by sharing my authentic thoughts and emotions during conversations. When I expressed vulnerability, I trusted in the promise of Proverbs 3:5-6: "Trust in the Lord with all your heart and lean not on your own understanding; in all your ways submit to Him, and He will make your paths straight."

Practical Tip: In your next conversation, practice sharing your genuine thoughts. Speak with love, and let the Spirit guide your words.

Practical Steps to Embrace Self-Expression

- **Explore Creative Outlets**
  Experiment with writing, music, art, or dance to discover the medium that resonates most with your spirit.

- **Create Without Judgment**
  Release the need for perfection or validation. Trust that the Spirit moves through your expression.

- **Reflect on Your Creations**
  Take time to contemplate what your creations reveal about your inner self.

- **Share with Love**
  When you're ready, share your expressions with others, trusting that vulnerability invites connection and understanding.

Mindfulness Integration

Mindfulness is the practice of paying attention to the present moment without judgment. It fosters self-awareness and emotional regulation and is essential for reducing stress, improving mental well-being, and enhancing well-being relationships.

Mindfulness involves gently directing your awareness to the present moment, observing thoughts, feelings, and sensations as they arise without becoming overwhelmed by them. It is a practice that fosters self-awareness and reflection, allowing you to better understand your thoughts and emotions. Mindfulness is not about attempting to change or control your experiences, but rather about observing and accepting them.

Before engaging in any creative practice:

- Pause and take a deep breath.
- Set the intention to let the Spirit guide your expression.
- Be fully present, releasing all judgment.

Key Takeaway

Self-expression is a divine gift, a sacred path to authenticity, self-discovery, and connection. By embracing creative and communicative outlets, you honor your Creator's handiwork and live in alignment with your highest truth. Let your life reflect the words of Ephesians 2:10: "For we are God's handiwork, created in Christ Jesus to do good works." Express yourself freely; your authentic self is a beacon of light to the world.

Remember that the most important aspect of being truly authentic is being fully yourself just for you – regardless of the outcome. You know who you are, what you think, what you feel, and what you stand for. That's more important than whether you choose to share it with others. However, when you do express it outwardly, celebrate and appreciate yourself for your efforts to be authentic.

When embarking on the journey to true authenticity, remember to bring along both your courage and discernment. Be mindful, watch for possible reactivity, and understand that authenticity can include setting boundaries. When expressing yourself, ask yourself the questions of what and how much, when and with whom, and what your desired result is. It's OK to share unabashedly, and it's also OK to allow silence as an option. With these tools, you'll uncover your genuine authenticity, no matter the circumstances.

Part 4

Living Authentically in the World

Chapter 10

Building Authentic Relationships

A uthentic relationships are the cornerstone of a life filled with joy, support, and personal growth. These relationships thrive when built on mutual respect, trust, and vulnerability. By embracing your true self, you invite others to do the same, fostering deeply enriching and enduring bonds. As you navigate your journey, remember that relationships are a divine gift meant to reflect God's love and purpose in our lives.

For example, romantic love is a gift of God's common grace intended for our enjoyment, and it is good when this type of love evolves into marriage. Biblical love belongs to a different category altogether. Biblical love is selfless, committed to truth, and driven by a divine work within us.

God, by His nature, exists in a righteous relationship, and He has created His image-bearers to do the same. Not only do relationships serve to sanctify us, but they also display it. The easiest way for us to observe our growth in Christ is to closely watch how we interact with, treat, and love others.

Family: Embracing Vulnerability

In my family, I once carried the weight of always appearing strong. I feared that sharing my struggles might diminish how they viewed me. Yet, this emotional distance hindered the love and connection we were meant to share.

As I started to share my fears and challenges, I experienced a transformation. Vulnerability became a bridge that brought us closer, and I saw the truth in Ecclesiastes 4:9-10: *"Two are better than one because they have a good return for their labor. If either of them falls down, one can help the other up."* As I shared, my family responded with empathy and understanding, deepening our bond in ways I never imagined.

Key Insight

Vulnerability isn't a sign of weakness; it's a doorway to deeper connection and love. It involves the willingness to reveal our true selves, acknowledge our imperfections, and embrace the unknown. By allowing ourselves to be vulnerable with others, we open the door to genuine and meaningful connections.

Friendships: Building Trust Through Honesty

For years, fearing conflict or rejection, I hesitated to share my true feelings with friends. However, true friendship, like love, "does not delight in evil but rejoices with the truth" (1 Corinthians 13:6). When I started speaking my mind honestly, even in difficult conversations, I discovered that trust flourished. Friends valued my authenticity, and our relationships deepened.

Key Insight

Honesty builds trust. By sharing your truth, you allow your friends to know and appreciate you genuinely. When you express your true thoughts, feelings, and experiences, your friends gain a more complete and accurate understanding of who you are. Authenticity fosters stronger, more meaningful relationships, enabling a deeper level of trust and understanding between individuals and friends.

By being open and honest, you allow your friends to appreciate you for who you truly are, not just for the facade you show to the world. Sharing your truth can feel vulnerable, but it is also a powerful way to connect with others and show courage. Open communication and honesty foster mutual growth and understanding in a friendship, enabling both parties to learn and evolve.

Romantic Relationships: Establishing Mutual Respect

In Ephesians 5:33: *"Each one of you also must love his wife as he loves himself, and the wife must respect her husband."* By openly discussing boundaries and expectations with my partner, I created a partnership where both of us feel seen, valued, and loved.

Key Insight

Mutual respect is the foundation of authentic love. Both partners must feel free to express their needs and emotions. Establishing clear boundaries and expectations is crucial in healthy relationships for fostering trust, respect, and mutual understanding while preventing misunderstandings and conflicts.

Healthy boundaries are also essential for maintaining a strong sense of self. They allow you to understand your values, limits, and triggers. Ultimately, they enable you to make conscious choices that align with your authentic self and protect your well-being. Knowing your boundaries allows you to make decisions that align with your values and what's truly important to you rather than being swayed by external pressures.

Professional Relationships: Encouraging Open Communication

In my career, I believed professionalism required suppressing personal experiences. Over time, I observed colleagues who shared appropriate personal stories, building stronger teams. This mirrored the wisdom of Proverbs 27:17: *"As iron sharpens iron, so one person sharpens another."*

I began sharing parts of my journey, which inspired open communication and created a supportive work environment. To further promote open communication and establish a nurturing work environment, I prioritized clear and consistent communication, encouraged active listening, provided constructive feedback, and fostered a culture of trust and respect.

As a leader, I consistently share information, solicit feedback, and remain open to differing perspectives. Of course, actions speak louder than words, so I make every effort to demonstrate the behaviors, attitudes, and values I expect from my team members. To foster a culture of trust and respect, I create a safe space to ensure team members feel comfortable expressing their ideas, concerns, and opinions without fear of judgment retaliation.

Encouraging open dialogue and actively listening to diverse viewpoints creates an environment where everyone feels valued and respected, regardless of their background or identity. By using various communication tools, such as instant messaging, email, team meetings, and project management platforms, this approach can meet the different needs and preferences of my team.

Here are some other strategies I use:

- **Establish clear communication protocols:** Define expectations for how and when information should be shared, ensuring everyone is on the same page.

- **Encourage regular feedback:** Implement regular check-ins and feedback sessions to facilitate open dialogue and address any issues promptly.
- **Practice active listening:** Pay close attention to what others say, ask clarifying questions, and summarize their points to ensure understanding.
- **Promote teamwork and collaboration:** Encourage employees to work together, share ideas, and support each other.
- **Celebrate successes and milestones:** Acknowledge and celebrate both individual and team accomplishments to boost morale and motivation.
- **Create a process for conflict resolution:** Establish clear procedures for addressing disagreements and conflicts in a respectful and constructive manner.
- **Encourage empathy and understanding:** Help employees understand different perspectives and find common ground.
- **Focus on solutions:** Encourage employees to work together to find solutions rather than assigning blame.
- **Promote a healthy work-life balance:** Encourage employees to take breaks, use their vacation time, and engage in activities outside of work.
- **Provide opportunities for development:** Offer training, mentorship, and other opportunities for employees to grow their skills and advance their careers.
- **Recognize and reward contributions:** Acknowledge and reward employees for their hard work and achievements.

Key Insight

Authenticity at work fosters collaboration and trust. Your genuine self inspires others to do the same. Trust naturally develops when individuals feel that their colleagues are genuine and transparent. This trust makes team members feel more comfortable sharing ideas, taking risks, and collaborating effectively.

Practical Steps to Foster Authentic Relationships with Examples

Practice Vulnerability

Share your authentic feelings and experiences with those you trust. Vulnerability nurtures understanding and connection.

Example: Share a recent challenge with a family member and observe how it strengthens your bond.

Communicate Openly

Speak your truth with kindness and respect, even when it's difficult.

Example: Share your honest perspective during a disagreement with a friend, and listen to theirs with an open heart.

Establish Boundaries

Healthy boundaries protect relationships from resentment and imbalance.

Example: Let a colleague know your limits while offering alternative ways to support.

Listen Actively

Active listening is a cornerstone of authentic relationships. Give others your full attention without judgment.

Example: In a conversation with a loved one, focus entirely on their words, tone, and emotions.

Be Consistent

Reliability builds trust. Align your actions with your words to demonstrate integrity.

Example: Honor your small or large promises to reinforce your credibility.

The Impact of Authentic Relationships

When you embrace authenticity, your relationships become a source of strength and joy.

- **Stronger Bonds:** Vulnerability fosters deeper connections.
- **Fulfillment:** Honest interactions align with your values.
- **Resilience:** Supportive relationships become your foundation in life's storms.

Practical Exercise

Reflect on a Significant Relationship

Choose one relationship in your life and reflect on the following:

- How authentic are you in this connection?
- What steps can you take to nurture greater authenticity?
- Is there a topic you are struggling to bring up and discuss?

Example: If you've been avoiding discussing personal struggles with a close friend, share something meaningful to foster understanding. Starting a conversation about personal struggles with a friend, especially if you've been avoiding it, can feel daunting. Start by reminding your friend how much you value their friendship and that your desire to share is rooted in that connection. Let them know you've been hesitant but that you want to be more open with them.

Find a private, comfortable setting where you can have an uninterrupted conversation. Avoid public or distracting places. Ensure both of you have ample time to talk without feeling rushed. You could even suggest a walk or grabbing coffee to create a relaxed atmosphere. Be clear, direct, and honest. Prepare what you want to say in advance, including how you would phrase it.

For example, use "I" statements to express feelings and experiences without blame. For instance, instead of saying, "You never listen," try, "I've been feeling unheard lately when I try to share my struggles." Clearly explain your needs and limits. Share your perspective and feelings, but don't feel pressured to offer solutions or advice. Remember, opening up is about creating a space for mutual understanding and empathy. Keep in mind that opening up is a process, and it may take time for both of you to adjust. By being patient, compassionate, and understanding, the conversation can strengthen the friendship and foster deeper understanding.

Mindfulness Integration

Incorporate mindfulness into your relationships:

- **Be Present:** Set aside distractions and focus fully on the person you're engaging with.
- **Respond with Empathy:** Acknowledge their feelings and share your thoughts sincerely.
- **Celebrate Connection:** Appreciate the beauty of the bond you're nurturing.

Key Takeaway

Authentic relationships reflect divine love built on honesty, respect, and vulnerability. By showing up as your true self, you create bonds that are not only enduring but also deeply fulfilling.

Chapter 11

Navigating Challenges and Setbacks

Challenges and setbacks are a natural part of life's journey, especially as we strive to live authentically. They test our resilience, sharpen our character, and reveal untapped potential within us. While these moments may be difficult, they offer an opportunity to grow, learn, and deepen our connection with our true selves. Drawing inspiration from Joseph Murphy's teachings, we'll explore how aligning our thoughts, faith, and actions with divine principles can empower us to face adversity with grace and purpose.

Additionally, scriptural wisdom will serve as a guiding light, reminding us that every trial can be a stepping stone to growth. Instead of viewing trials as solely negative experiences, this perspective encourages seeing them as opportunities for learning, development, and strengthening one's character.

Overcoming challenges can build resilience and teach us to navigate adversity with greater strength and determination. Each trial offers valuable lessons and insights, leading to a deeper understanding of ourselves and our capabilities. By reframing trials as stepping stones, we can move from a place of fear and resistance to empowerment and growth.

The truth is simple: Spiritual growth involves movement, progression, and change. However, change for change's sake is not the point. God's plan for us is growth with purpose. Suffering doesn't define us; it shapes who we are. Healing isn't about erasing pain but about finding strength beyond it. We all face struggles that test us, but our suffering is not our identity—it's part of our journey. True healing isn't about forgetting or pretending the pain never existed; it's about discovering resilience, growth, and the strength to move forward.

Embracing Self-Compassion During Professional Setbacks

Early in my career, I faced a professional failure that shook my confidence. A project I passionately led fell short of expectations, and the disappointment consumed me. My inner dialogue was harsh and critical, undermining my sense of worth.

The Shift: Through the teachings of self-compassion, I replaced self-condemnation with kindness. I affirmed: *"I am guided by divine wisdom, and every experience leads to my growth."* I reflected on Romans 8:28: *"And we know that in all things God works for the good of those who love him."* This reminded me that my efforts could be redirected for a greater purpose, even in failure.

Key Insight

When setbacks occur, practice self-compassion. Forgive yourself and affirm that every challenge holds a hidden blessing, leading you closer to your purpose. Self-compassion is about showing yourself the same acceptance and understanding that you would show a friend or loved one when facing setbacks. It's a practice that feeds more life into your physical body and mental and emotional health. But it's also a practice that takes continuous work.

Cultivating Resilience Amid Personal Losses

The sudden loss of a close friend left me feeling vulnerable and unsteady. Grief clouded my days, and I struggled to find meaning in the pain I was experiencing.

The Shift: Turning to spiritual guidance, I prayed for strength and clarity. As I meditated on James 1:2-4 *"Consider it pure joy, my brothers and sisters, whenever you face trials of many kinds..."* I began to see grief not as an endpoint but as a transformation. By cherishing the memories and leaning on my support network, I honored the loss and the enduring love that remained.

Key Insight

Resilience isn't about erasing pain but about transforming it. Trust that God's strength within you can guide you through the darkest valleys into new light. Instead of viewing scars as signs of weakness, they can be seen as badges of honor, representing the battles fought and the strength developed. Transforming pain can lead to a deeper understanding of oneself and a sense of purpose, allowing individuals to find meaning in their struggles. True resilience isn't about suppressing emotions or "powering through" without pausing to reflect or heal.

Adapting to Unexpected Changes in Personal Relationships

A long-standing friendship began to fade as our life paths diverged. I clung to what once was, feeling unsettled by the change.

The Shift: I turned inward, aligning my heart with Proverbs 3:5-6: "Trust in the Lord with all your heart and lean not on your own understanding; in all your ways submit to him, and he will make your paths straight." By releasing my attachment to the past, I welcomed new opportunities for growth. Joining a book club introduced me to like-minded individuals, and volunteering offered fulfillment, new experiences, and friendships.

Key Insight

Life's transitions are divine invitations to align more deeply with your true self. Trust the process and remain open to new connections and experiences.

Many of us try to "control" everything around us, including our finances, careers, relationships, schedules, bodies, and perhaps even our church experiences. Much of our negativity and resistance to change often revolves around this overwhelming desire for control, sometimes approaching idolatry

Perhaps you have struggled with anxious thoughts and behaviors or have experienced a situation in which you were subject to trauma or loss. Whatever has imprinted upon our hearts and minds, our spirits are naturally resolute to stick to what we consider comfortable and safe.

Practical Strategies for Navigating Challenges

Practice Self-Compassion

Replace negative self-talk with affirmations rooted in divine truth.

Example: When you feel overwhelmed by a mistake, affirm: *"I am a child of God, learning and growing with each step."*

Build Resilience

Strengthen your mind, body, and spirit through meditation, exercise, and prayer.

Example: Reflect daily on a scripture that inspires you, such as Philippians 4:13: *"I can do all things through Christ who strengthens me."*

Embrace Adaptability

View changes as divine redirections, leading you closer to your purpose.

Example: When a door closes, affirm: *"God opens new doors of opportunity and growth for me."*

Reflect and Learn

Ask: *What is God teaching me through this experience?* Journaling or quiet reflection can reveal valuable lessons.

Stay True to Yourself

Let authenticity be your anchor. Align your actions with your values and faith.

Example: When facing criticism, stand firm in your convictions, affirming: *"God is my guide, and I trust His plan for me."*

Practical Exercise

Reflect on a Recent Setback:

1. Identify a challenge you've faced recently.
2. Write down how you reacted and how it made you feel.
3. Ask: *How can I reframe this experience as an opportunity for growth?*
4. Pray or meditate on James 1:2-4, inviting divine guidance into your reflections

To turn challenges into opportunities for growth, adopt a growth mindset that sees obstacles as chances to learn and improve rather than roadblocks. This involves changing your perspective, focusing on what you can control, and seeking solutions instead of dwelling on the problem. By reframing challenges, you can build resilience, develop new skills, and ultimately achieve personal and professional growth.

_____

_____

_____

_____

_____

_____

Mindfulness Integration

When adversity strikes, integrate mindful acceptance with prayer:

Sit quietly, breathing deeply. Acknowledge your feelings without judgment, affirming: *"God's peace surrounds me."*Invite clarity by meditating on a scripture, such as Psalm 46:10: *"Be still, and know that I am God."*

Key Takeaway

Challenges are not detours but divine lessons. You strengthen your faith and authenticity by practicing self-compassion, resilience, and adaptability. Trust that God's plan is unfolding perfectly, even when the path feels uncertain. Life is unpredictable, but God's character never changes. He is faithful, good, and working all things for His glory and your good – even when you can't see it.

As Lamentations 3:22-23 says, "His mercies are new every morning; great is Your faithfulness." When the world feels shaky, hold tight to the Rock that never moves. Lean into His promises, surround yourself with community, and rest in the truth that He is working all things for your good. Let's trust Him together, one uncertain day at a time.

Chapter 12

Maintaining Authenticity in a Changing World

A uthenticity is not a fixed point—it is a continuous journey that calls for reflection, growth, and the ability to adapt. In a constantly evolving world, the challenge of staying true to oneself may seem overwhelming, yet it also presents an invaluable opportunity to connect more deeply with your true values and aspirations. "Jesus Christ is the same yesterday and today and forever" (Hebrews 13:8), and in this ever-changing world, we can find solace in the consistency of our divine purpose.

In this chapter, we'll explore how practices such as self-reflection, self-compassion, and adaptability enable us to preserve our authenticity amid the shifting tides of life. Through personal reflections and actionable strategies, I will guide you on how to stay aligned with your core self as you navigate change, finding strength in God's unwavering guidance.

Embracing Career Transitions with Self-Reflection

Career changes often evoke uncertainty but also offer profound opportunities for growth and alignment with your deeper purpose. When we experience discomfort in our current path, it is a sign to reflect, just as the Psalmist wrote: "Be still, and know that I am God" (Psalm 46:10).

My Journey

After several years of working in informatics, I felt a growing disconnect between my daily tasks and my true calling. This realization led me to a period of deep reflection. I prayed for clarity and revisited my passions and long-term goals. I discovered a desire to make a more direct impact on patient care, a calling that had been obscured by my technical responsibilities.

The Shift: With renewed purpose, I transitioned into healthcare, where I could combine my technical skills with patient-centered care. This decision required further education and the courage to step out of my comfort zone, but the rewards—a career deeply aligned with my values—were worth every challenge.

Key Insight

Reflection is a sacred tool. By taking the time to pause, assess your values, and realign your goals, you position yourself to live according to God's purpose for your life. Reflection is a deeper form of learning that enables us to retain every aspect of any experience, whether personal or professional—why something occurred, what the impact was, and whether it should happen again—rather than just remembering that it happened.

Practicing Self-Compassion During Personal Challenges

Transitions are often laden with obstacles. During my career shift, I encountered moments of doubt and fear of failure. However, I learned to lean into self-compassion, an essential practice that provided me with the resilience to continue. Philippians 4:6-7 teaches us, "Do not be anxious about anything, but in every situation, by prayer and petition, with thanksgiving, present your requests to God."

The Shift: I reminded myself that pursuing my passion required courage. I embraced the notion that growth is rarely linear and that mistakes are part of the learning process. Self-compassion transformed my moments of self-doubt into opportunities for resilience, grounded in God's grace.

Key Insight

Self-compassion is a stabilizing force. It allows you to be patient with yourself, recognizing that perfection is not the goal— progress is. We can lean on God's unwavering love and mercy as we navigate change. Self-compassion is like being a good friend to yourself. Think about a time when you supported a friend, helped a colleague, or comforted a child. You probably showed empathy, not pity, and recognized that life can be tough and imperfect. Self-compassion is about treating yourself with the same kindness and understanding.

Adapting Social Connections in a Digital Era

The global pandemic illuminated the importance of adaptability in maintaining meaningful relationships. Initially, I resisted virtual interactions, longing for the richness of face-to-face connection. Over time, I came to realize that embracing digital platforms was essential for preserving my relationships, much like how we adapt to God's plan even when it doesn't unfold in ways we expect. In other words, people create many plans for themselves throughout their life. However, these plans will only come to fruition if it is the Lord's will and if it is part of His plan for you.

I'm a firm believer that everything happens for a reason and that everything you endure is part of God's plan for you. I know it can be nerve-wracking not knowing why things are happening to you, where you're headed, or what your future holds, but my greatest piece of advice is to completely trust that God will guide you and take care of you. As Proverbs 3:5-6 says, *"Trust in the Lord with all your heart, and do not lean on your own understanding. In all your ways acknowledge him, and he will make straight your paths."* I hope that this helps you not only to put greater trust in God, but also to grow closer to Him.

The Shift: I embraced online gatherings, joined virtual communities, and found creative ways to stay connected with loved ones. These efforts allowed me to preserve the authenticity of my relationships, even during physical separation. Call to catch up or send a quick text to share something that made you think of them. Let them know how important they are to you. Even a simple note saying, "How are you?" or "I'm glad you are in my life" will let them know that you care about them and keep the connection current.

Key Insight

Adaptability is key to thriving in changing circumstances. By finding new ways to connect, you can maintain the essence of authenticity, knowing that God's plans are always unfolding, whether through virtual or physical means.

The ability to pivot, learn quickly, and adjust to new circumstances makes you more resilient in times of crisis. Whether it's changing careers, moving to a new city, or navigating personal challenges, adaptability gives you the tools to thrive.

Practical Strategies for Sustaining Authenticity
Regular Self-Reflection

Take time to check in with yourself. Reflect on your values, goals, and experiences through journaling or prayer, continually aligning them with God's purpose. *Example:* Dedicate 10 minutes daily to write about your thoughts and feelings. Reflect on how your actions align with your core values and God's calling for you.

Cultivate Self-Compassion

Be kind to yourself, especially during times of change. Recognize your efforts and offer forgiveness for your imperfections. *Example:* When faced with setbacks, say, "I am doing my best, and growth takes time." Remember that God's grace is ever-present, guiding you forward.

Embrace Adaptability

Life is fluid, and staying flexible allows you to move through change while remaining true to yourself. For example, if a long-term goal no longer aligns with your values, pivot with faith and trust that God is guiding your path.

Seek Supportive Communities

Surround yourself with individuals who encourage and respect your authentic self. Engage in communities that align with your values. *Example:* Join a group or fellowship that supports your personal growth, whether through a Bible study group, a professional network, or a volunteer organization.

Commit to Lifelong Learning

Every experience is a divine opportunity for growth. Approach life with curiosity and a willingness to evolve. *Example:* Take a course or pursue a skill that aligns with your interests and goals, always seeking to grow in alignment with God's purpose.

Practical Exercise

Develop a Personal Action Plan

Create a plan for maintaining authenticity in different areas of your life. Consider these prompts:

Work: *How can you ensure your career aligns with your values?*

Example: Set aside time each year to evaluate your career goals in light of your core values.

Relationships: *What steps can you take to nurture authentic connections?*

Example: Commit to honest, open communication with loved ones, grounded in love and respect.

Personal Growth: *How will you prioritize self-reflection and learning?*

Example: Schedule regular time for journaling or mindfulness practices to strengthen your connection with God and your true self.

Challenges, when viewed through a lens of faith, can be reframed as opportunities for spiritual growth and deeper reliance on God. By embracing difficulties with a mindset of learning and trusting in God's plan, individuals can develop resilience, maturity, and a stronger connection with their faith. This reframing involves recognizing that trials can refine character, build perseverance, and ultimately lead to a more Christ-like nature.

_____

_____

_____

_____

_____

_____

Mindfulness Integration

Regular mindfulness practice strengthens self-awareness and adaptability:

Breath Awareness: Spend five minutes focusing on your breath. Let each inhale ground you in the present moment, and each exhale release any tension.

Gratitude Reflection: Reflect on the aspects of your life that align with your authentic self. This gratitude practice reinforces your sense of purpose and direction, acknowledging that every step forward is part of God's plan for you.

Key Takeaway

Authenticity is not a destination; it is a lifelong journey. It is not somewhere you simply arrive. Through self-reflection, self-compassion, and adaptability, you can navigate life's changes while staying true to yourself, continually aligning with God's perfect plan for your life. Just as "Jesus Christ is the same yesterday and today and forever" (Hebrews 13:8), so too is your path of authenticity grounded in an unchanging divine purpose.

True authenticity is unattached visibility. It takes confidence to evolve while expressing what feels true to you in any given moment, knowing that will likely change. If it doesn't change, that is where the real work comes in. No one can define what that is for you, so let 'now' be that moment. What does authenticity mean to you?

Conclusion

Embracing the Infinite Horizon of Authenticity

As we conclude *Embracing Your Authentic Self: A Journey to True Freedom,* let us recognize that authenticity is not a final destination or an achievement to check off a list. It is a lifelong, evolving journey—a sacred dance between who you are today and who you are becoming. This journey beckons you to explore the depths of your soul, peel away the layers of societal expectations, and walk boldly in alignment with your innermost truth.

To live boldly means to embrace courage, take risks, and live authentically by pursuing your passions and desires, even when faced with uncertainty or potential challenges. It means:

- **Embracing Courage:** Living boldly requires facing fears and stepping outside of comfort zones. It means taking action, even when the outcome is uncertain or potentially difficult.
- **Taking Risks:** Bold living involves taking chances and putting yourself out there, whether it's starting a new business, pursuing a passion project, or speaking up for what you believe in.
- **Authenticity:** Living boldly means being true to yourself and your values, rather than conforming to societal expectations or pressures.
- **Pursuing What Matters:** It's about identifying what truly matters to you and actively working towards those goals, even when faced with setbacks or obstacles.

- **Overcoming Fear:** Bold living often involves confronting and overcoming personal fears, such as fear of failure, rejection, or the unknown.
- **Living on your own terms:** It means tuning into your own needs and desires and deciding what you want out of life.

Throughout these chapters, we have navigated the terrains of self-discovery, courage, vulnerability, and connection. We've challenged perfection, dismantled conditioning, and reclaimed the beauty of imperfection. We've ventured into the liberating realms of self-compassion, resilience, and authentic relationships. Each step, no matter how small, moves you closer to the freedom of living unapologetically as yourself.

The Power of Your Authenticity

To live authentically is to honor the divine masterpiece that is your life. Your imperfections, quirks, dreams, and struggles are all threads in a tapestry woven with purpose. Authenticity is not about being flawless; it's about being whole. It's about standing firmly in the truth of who you are, even when the world pressures you to conform. It's about shedding the masks you've worn for survival and daring to show up as your most vulnerable, radiant self.

Authenticity is your gift to the world. When you live from a place of truth, you inspire others to do the same. You create ripples of freedom and courage in your relationships, your community, and beyond. Your authentic life becomes a beacon, illuminating the path for others seeking their own liberation.

Embrace the Journey Ahead

Life is ever-changing, and so too is your journey toward authenticity. There will be moments of clarity and moments of doubt, triumphs that fill your heart and challenges that test your resolve. In every season, let your authenticity ground you. When faced with uncertainty, return to your values. When fear whispers, counter it with self-compassion. When you stumble, rise with the wisdom gained from the fall.

Remember, authenticity is not a solitary endeavor. It flourishes in connection. Surround yourself with those who celebrate your truth and challenge you to grow. Seek spaces where your voice is heard and your presence is valued. And when the weight of the world feels heavy, know that your authenticity is enough—it always has been and always will be.

Step into Your Freedom

Living authentically is the greatest act of courage you can undertake. It liberates you from the constraints of "should" and "must" and opens the door to a life of meaning, joy, and alignment. It transforms ordinary moments into profound experiences and infuses your life with a sense of divine purpose.

In the words of Maya Angelou, *"You alone are enough. You have nothing to prove to anybody."* Let these words be your mantra as you step boldly into the freedom of your authentic self.

Here's a deeper look at the meaning and impact of this quote:

- **Self-Sufficiency and Value:** The core message is that your worth is intrinsic and doesn't depend on external achievements or the opinions of others. You are complete and valuable simply by virtue of being.
- **Rejection of Validation Seeking:** The quote encourages you to stop seeking validation from others and instead focus on your own inner strength and self-acceptance.
- **Empowerment and Self-Love:** It's a powerful reminder to embrace your individuality and to have confidence in your own abilities and worth.

- **Resilience and Self-compassion:** The quote can be particularly helpful in times of doubt or self-criticism, reminding you that you are enough and that you don't need to constantly prove yourself to others.

A Blessing for Your Journey

As you continue on this journey, may you find the strength to honor your truth, the grace to embrace your imperfections, and the courage to shine your light in the world. May you walk this path with curiosity, resilience, and an open heart, knowing that each step brings you closer to the fullness of who you are meant to be.

This book has been more than a guide—it has been a labor of love, a testament to the power of authenticity to heal, transform, and liberate. As you close these pages, know that your journey is just beginning. The world needs your unique voice, your unrepeatable story, and your unapologetic truth.

Live boldly.

Love deeply.

And always, always embrace the beautiful, imperfect, and extraordinary gift of being authentically you.

Go forth and live your freedom.

The world is waiting.

About the Author

Dr. Vivian Tantoh Mondo

D r. Vivian Tantoh Mondo, DNP, is a dedicated psychiatric nurse practitioner, a trailblazer in mental health advocacy, and a living testament to resilience, purpose, and authenticity. As the founder of a thriving practice, a mother of three remarkable children, a devoted pastor's wife, and the proud eldest child of her family, Dr. Mondo's life is a dynamic tapestry woven with lessons in leadership, empathy, and unwavering faith.

Growing up as the firstborn in her family, Dr. Mondo was entrusted with responsibility and leadership from an early age. Guided by her parents' emphasis on discipline, integrity, and excellence, she cultivated the values that would shape her life's purpose. However, her path was indelibly marked by loss. The passing of her mother at 17, followed closely by her father's death, became a crucible of grief and transformation. These profound experiences deepened her empathy and ignited a determination to channel her pain into purpose, inspiring her commitment to make a meaningful impact in the lives of others.

Dr. Mondo's journey into psychiatric nursing was not a linear one but a calling born from her keen awareness of the silent struggles that individuals and families often endure. Witnessing the pervasive stigma surrounding mental health, she felt a profound urge to be part of the solution. Pursuing advanced education and establishing her own practice were milestones not only of professional achievement but also of service—offering compassionate care, advocating for mental health awareness, and challenging societal misconceptions about mental illness.

Beyond her professional achievements, Dr. Mondo's life is deeply enriched by her role as a mother. Parenting three unique children has been both a grounding force and an ongoing education in patience, unconditional love, and balance. Her children are her daily inspiration, reminding her of the importance of embracing one's authentic self and finding joy in imperfection.

As a pastor's wife, Dr. Mondo is honored to serve alongside her husband in ministry. This role has allowed her to witness the transformative power of faith in people's lives and to provide support through counseling, mentoring, and encouragement. Her spiritual foundation is the compass guiding her decisions, fostering her commitment to serving others and living authentically.

Navigating the intersection of her personal and professional roles has not been without challenges. Moments of fatigue, doubt, and the quest for balance have tested her resolve, but they have also been profound teachers. These experiences have reinforced the importance of self-reflection, self-compassion, and the courage to embrace one's imperfections. For Dr. Mondo, authenticity means honoring both strengths and vulnerabilities, finding grace in the journey, and standing firmly in the truth that she is enough.

Her passion for authenticity fuels her writing and advocacy. Dr. Mondo believes that the journey to self-discovery is an act of courage and faith—one that requires peeling back the layers of societal expectations and fears to uncover the essence of who we are. It is a process of liberation and empowerment, and one she hopes to inspire in others.

Embracing Your Authentic Self is more than a book; it is an invitation. Dr. Mondo invites readers to reflect on their own journeys, to shed the weight of external expectations, and to step boldly into the beauty of living unapologetically. With faith, courage, and self-discovery, she believes we can create a world where authenticity is celebrated and each person feels empowered to live their truth.

This is Dr. Vivian Tantoh Mondo's story; through her words, she extends her hand to walk with you on your path toward freedom, healing, and transformation.

Your Journey Continues

Congratulations on taking this transformative journey toward authentic living! You've done the courageous work of looking inward, challenging limiting beliefs, and embracing your true self. But remember—this is just the beginning.

Your authentic life is waiting, and you don't have to walk this path alone.

Connect with Dr. Vivian

I invite you to continue this journey of growth and discovery by connecting with our community of authentic living enthusiasts:

- **Visit my website:** DrVivianMondo.com for additional resources, blog posts, and inspiration to support your ongoing transformation.
- **Join the conversation:** Follow me on social media @ DrVivianMondo for encouragement, authentic living tips, and behind-the-scenes glimpses of this beautiful, imperfect journey we're all on.

Share Your Story

Your authentic journey matters. I'd love to hear how this book has impacted your life. Share your story, insights, or questions.

Remember: You are enough. You are worthy. You are called to live boldly.

The world needs your unique light. Keep shining.

With love and encouragement,
Dr. Vivian Tantoh Mondo

References

Foster, A. (n.d.). Journey to freedom: Discovering your authentic self while overcoming isolation and fearful thoughts. Retrieved from https://www.amazon.com/Journey-Freedom-Discovering-Authentic-Overcoming/dp/B0DJ2LB592

Grace, S. (2023). Embrace your authentic self: A guide to living your truth. Retrieved from https://www.barnesandnoble.com/w/embrace-your-authentic-self-serena-grace/1146341375

Bjelland, J. (2023). Breaking free from perfection: Embracing your authentic self. Retrieved from https://www.juliebjelland.com/hsp-blog/breaking-free-from-perfection-embracing-your-authentic-self-by-julie-bjelland-lmft

Hill, T. (2023). The journey to authenticity: Embracing your true self. Retrieved from https://www.barnesandnoble.com/w/the-journey-to-authenticity-tanya-hill/1146050245

Singer, M. A. (2007). The untethered soul: The journey beyond yourself. Oakland, CA: New Harbinger Publications.

Brown, B. (2010). The gifts of imperfection: Let go of who you think you're supposed to be and embrace who you are. Center City, MN: Hazelden Publishing.

Brown, B. (2012). Daring greatly: How the courage to be vulnerable transforms the way we live, love, parent, and lead. New York, NY: Gotham Books.

Ruiz, D. M. (1997). The four agreements: A practical guide to personal freedom. San Rafael, CA: Amber-Allen Publishing.

Spade, D. (2025). Love in a fcked up world: How to build relationships, hook up, and raise hell together*. Retrieved from https://www.teenvogue.com/story/dean-spade-love-in-world-qa

Ferrell, K. (2025). You'll never believe me. Retrieved from https://pagesix.com/2025/01/07/style/hipster-grifter-kari-ferrell-on-the-six-books-that-make-her-feel-seen/

www.ingramcontent.com/pod-product-compliance
Lightning Source LLC
Chambersburg PA
CBHW071312130626
46556CB00004B/1575